TODDLER
DAILY LOG BOOK

Copyright © 2021 Allayas Inc.

All rights reserved. No part of this publication may be reproduced, distributed, or transmitted without prior written permission of the publisher, except as provided by United States of America copyright law. For official permission requests, write to the publisher, at allayasinc@gmail.com with the subject line: "Attention: Permissions Coordinator."

www.allayas.com

TODDLER REPORT

CHILD'S NAME:

DATE:

Ⓢ Ⓜ Ⓣ Ⓦ Ⓣ Ⓕ Ⓢ

MOOD:
- ☐ Chatty
- ☐ Happy
- ☐ Cranky
- ☐ Playful
- ☐ Cuddly
- ☐ Quiet
- ☐ Friendly
- ☐ Sad
- ☐ Fussy
- ☐ Sick
- ☐ Grumpy
- ☐ Sleepy
- ☐ Other: _____

NOTES FROM PARENT(S):
_____
_____
_____
_____

WOKE UP AT:
A.M.
P.M.

LAST FED AT:
A.M.
P.M.

MEALS:

	TIME
Breakfast	
Snack	
Lunch	
Snack	
Dinner	

POTTY:

Time	Diaper	Potty	Dry	Wet	BM
_____	☐	☐	☐	☐	☐
_____	☐	☐	☐	☐	☐
_____	☐	☐	☐	☐	☐
_____	☐	☐	☐	☐	☐
_____	☐	☐	☐	☐	☐
_____	☐	☐	☐	☐	☐
_____	☐	☐	☐	☐	☐

ACTIVITIES:
- ☐ FREE PLAY
- ☐ READING
- ☐ ARTS/CRAFTS
- ☐ MUSIC/SINGING
- ☐ OUTDOORS PLAY
- ☐ TV/MOVIE
- ☐ FIELD TRIP
- ☐ PLAYDATE WITH _____
- ☐ OTHER _____

SLEEP:

FROM	TO

ACCIDENT REPORT:

ACCIDENT	CARE GIVEN

MEDICATION(S):

TIME	TYPE	AMOUNT

SUPPLIES NEEDED:
_____
_____
_____
_____
_____

NOTES TO PARENTS:
_____
_____
_____
_____
_____

TIME IN: **TIME OUT:**

TODDLER REPORT

CHILD'S NAME:

DATE:

Ⓢ Ⓜ Ⓣ Ⓦ Ⓣ Ⓕ Ⓢ

MOOD:
- ☐ Chatty
- ☐ Happy
- ☐ Cranky
- ☐ Playful
- ☐ Cuddly
- ☐ Quiet
- ☐ Friendly
- ☐ Sad
- ☐ Fussy
- ☐ Sick
- ☐ Grumpy
- ☐ Sleepy
- ☐ Other: _____

NOTES FROM PARENT(S):

WOKE UP AT:
A.M.
P.M.

LAST FED AT:
A.M.
P.M.

MEALS:
	TIME
Breakfast	
Snack	
Lunch	
Snack	
Dinner	

POTTY:
Time	Diaper	Potty	Dry	Wet	BM
	☐	☐	☐	☐	☐
	☐	☐	☐	☐	☐
	☐	☐	☐	☐	☐
	☐	☐	☐	☐	☐
	☐	☐	☐	☐	☐
	☐	☐	☐	☐	☐
	☐	☐	☐	☐	☐

ACTIVITIES:
- ☐ FREE PLAY
- ☐ READING
- ☐ ARTS/CRAFTS
- ☐ MUSIC/SINGING
- ☐ OUTDOORS PLAY
- ☐ TV/MOVIE
- ☐ FIELD TRIP
- ☐ PLAYDATE WITH _____
- ☐ OTHER _____

SLEEP:
FROM	TO

ACCIDENT REPORT:
ACCIDENT	CARE GIVEN

MEDICATION(S):
TIME	TYPE	AMOUNT

SUPPLIES NEEDED:

NOTES TO PARENTS:

TIME IN: **TIME OUT:**

TODDLER REPORT

CHILD'S NAME:

DATE:

Ⓢ Ⓜ Ⓣ Ⓦ Ⓣ Ⓕ Ⓢ

MOOD:
- ☐ Chatty
- ☐ Happy
- ☐ Cranky
- ☐ Playful
- ☐ Cuddly
- ☐ Quiet
- ☐ Friendly
- ☐ Sad
- ☐ Fussy
- ☐ Sick
- ☐ Grumpy
- ☐ Sleepy
- ☐ Other: _____

NOTES FROM PARENT(S):
_____
_____
_____
_____
_____

WOKE UP AT:
A.M.
P.M.

LAST FED AT:
A.M.
P.M.

MEALS:

	TIME
Breakfast	
Snack	
Lunch	
Snack	
Dinner	

POTTY:

Time	Diaper	Potty	Dry	Wet	BM
___	☐	☐	☐	☐	☐
___	☐	☐	☐	☐	☐
___	☐	☐	☐	☐	☐
___	☐	☐	☐	☐	☐
___	☐	☐	☐	☐	☐
___	☐	☐	☐	☐	☐
___	☐	☐	☐	☐	☐

ACTIVITIES:
- ☐ FREE PLAY
- ☐ READING
- ☐ ARTS/CRAFTS
- ☐ MUSIC/SINGING
- ☐ OUTDOORS PLAY
- ☐ TV/MOVIE
- ☐ FIELD TRIP
- ☐ PLAYDATE WITH _____
- ☐ OTHER _____

SLEEP:

FROM	TO

ACCIDENT REPORT:

ACCIDENT	CARE GIVEN

MEDICATION(S):

TIME	TYPE	AMOUNT

SUPPLIES NEEDED:
_____
_____
_____
_____
_____

NOTES TO PARENTS:
_____
_____
_____
_____
_____

TIME IN: **TIME OUT:**

TODDLER REPORT

CHILD'S NAME:

DATE:

S M T W T F S

MOOD:
- ☐ Chatty
- ☐ Happy
- ☐ Cranky
- ☐ Playful
- ☐ Cuddly
- ☐ Quiet
- ☐ Friendly
- ☐ Sad
- ☐ Fussy
- ☐ Sick
- ☐ Grumpy
- ☐ Sleepy
- ☐ Other: _____

NOTES FROM PARENT(S):

WOKE UP AT:
A.M.
P.M.

LAST FED AT:
A.M.
P.M.

MEALS:

	TIME
Breakfast	
Snack	
Lunch	
Snack	
Dinner	

POTTY:

Time	Diaper	Potty	Dry	Wet	BM
	☐	☐	☐	☐	☐
	☐	☐	☐	☐	☐
	☐	☐	☐	☐	☐
	☐	☐	☐	☐	☐
	☐	☐	☐	☐	☐
	☐	☐	☐	☐	☐
	☐	☐	☐	☐	☐

ACTIVITIES:
- ☐ FREE PLAY
- ☐ READING
- ☐ ARTS/CRAFTS
- ☐ MUSIC/SINGING
- ☐ OUTDOORS PLAY
- ☐ TV/MOVIE
- ☐ FIELD TRIP
- ☐ PLAYDATE WITH _____
- ☐ OTHER _____

SLEEP:

FROM	TO

ACCIDENT REPORT:

ACCIDENT	CARE GIVEN

MEDICATION(S):

TIME	TYPE	AMOUNT

SUPPLIES NEEDED:

NOTES TO PARENTS:

TIME IN: **TIME OUT:**

TODDLER REPORT

DATE:

CHILD'S NAME:

S M T W T F S

MOOD:
- [ ] Chatty
- [ ] Happy
- [ ] Cranky
- [ ] Playful
- [ ] Cuddly
- [ ] Quiet
- [ ] Friendly
- [ ] Sad
- [ ] Fussy
- [ ] Sick
- [ ] Grumpy
- [ ] Sleepy
- [ ] Other: _____

NOTES FROM PARENT(S):
_____
_____
_____
_____
_____

WOKE UP AT:
A.M.
P.M.

LAST FED AT:
A.M.
P.M.

MEALS:

	TIME
Breakfast	
Snack	
Lunch	
Snack	
Dinner	

POTTY:

Time	Diaper	Potty	Dry	Wet	BM
___	☐	☐	☐	☐	☐
___	☐	☐	☐	☐	☐
___	☐	☐	☐	☐	☐
___	☐	☐	☐	☐	☐
___	☐	☐	☐	☐	☐
___	☐	☐	☐	☐	☐
___	☐	☐	☐	☐	☐

ACTIVITIES:
- [ ] FREE PLAY
- [ ] READING
- [ ] ARTS/CRAFTS
- [ ] MUSIC/SINGING
- [ ] OUTDOORS PLAY
- [ ] TV/MOVIE
- [ ] FIELD TRIP
- [ ] PLAYDATE WITH _____
- [ ] OTHER _____

SLEEP:

FROM	TO

ACCIDENT REPORT:

ACCIDENT	CARE GIVEN

MEDICATION(S):

TIME	TYPE	AMOUNT

SUPPLIES NEEDED:
_____
_____
_____
_____
_____

NOTES TO PARENTS:
_____
_____
_____
_____
_____

TIME IN: **TIME OUT:**

TODDLER REPORT

DATE:

CHILD'S NAME:

Ⓢ Ⓜ Ⓣ Ⓦ Ⓣ Ⓕ Ⓢ

MOOD:
- ☐ Chatty
- ☐ Happy
- ☐ Cranky
- ☐ Playful
- ☐ Cuddly
- ☐ Quiet
- ☐ Friendly
- ☐ Sad
- ☐ Fussy
- ☐ Sick
- ☐ Grumpy
- ☐ Sleepy
- ☐ Other: _____

NOTES FROM PARENT(S):
_____
_____
_____
_____
_____

WOKE UP AT:
A.M.
P.M.

LAST FED AT:
A.M.
P.M.

MEALS:

	TIME
Breakfast	
Snack	
Lunch	
Snack	
Dinner	

POTTY:

Time	Diaper	Potty	Dry	Wet	BM
___	☐	☐	☐	☐	☐
___	☐	☐	☐	☐	☐
___	☐	☐	☐	☐	☐
___	☐	☐	☐	☐	☐
___	☐	☐	☐	☐	☐
___	☐	☐	☐	☐	☐
___	☐	☐	☐	☐	☐

ACTIVITIES:
- ☐ FREE PLAY
- ☐ READING
- ☐ ARTS/CRAFTS
- ☐ MUSIC/SINGING
- ☐ OUTDOORS PLAY
- ☐ TV/MOVIE
- ☐ FIELD TRIP
- ☐ PLAYDATE WITH _____
- ☐ OTHER _____

SLEEP:

FROM	TO

ACCIDENT REPORT:

ACCIDENT	CARE GIVEN

MEDICATION(S):

TIME	TYPE	AMOUNT

SUPPLIES NEEDED:
_____
_____
_____
_____
_____

NOTES TO PARENTS:
_____
_____
_____
_____
_____

TIME IN: **TIME OUT:**

TODDLER REPORT

CHILD'S NAME:

DATE:

Ⓢ Ⓜ Ⓣ Ⓦ Ⓣ Ⓕ Ⓢ

MOOD:
- ☐ Chatty
- ☐ Happy
- ☐ Cranky
- ☐ Playful
- ☐ Cuddly
- ☐ Quiet
- ☐ Friendly
- ☐ Sad
- ☐ Fussy
- ☐ Sick
- ☐ Grumpy
- ☐ Sleepy
- ☐ Other: _____

NOTES FROM PARENT(S):
_____
_____
_____
_____

WOKE UP AT:
A.M.
P.M.

LAST FED AT:
A.M.
P.M.

MEALS:

	TIME
Breakfast	
Snack	
Lunch	
Snack	
Dinner	

POTTY:

Time	Diaper	Potty	Dry	Wet	BM
___	☐	☐	☐	☐	☐
___	☐	☐	☐	☐	☐
___	☐	☐	☐	☐	☐
___	☐	☐	☐	☐	☐
___	☐	☐	☐	☐	☐
___	☐	☐	☐	☐	☐
___	☐	☐	☐	☐	☐

ACTIVITIES:
- ☐ FREE PLAY
- ☐ READING
- ☐ ARTS/CRAFTS
- ☐ MUSIC/SINGING
- ☐ OUTDOORS PLAY
- ☐ TV/MOVIE
- ☐ FIELD TRIP
- ☐ PLAYDATE WITH _____
- ☐ OTHER _____

SLEEP:

FROM	TO

ACCIDENT REPORT:

ACCIDENT	CARE GIVEN

MEDICATION(S):

TIME	TYPE	AMOUNT

SUPPLIES NEEDED:
_____
_____
_____
_____
_____

NOTES TO PARENTS:
_____
_____
_____
_____
_____

TIME IN: **TIME OUT:**

TODDLER REPORT

CHILD'S NAME:

DATE:

Ⓢ Ⓜ Ⓣ Ⓦ Ⓣ Ⓕ Ⓢ

MOOD:
- ☐ Chatty
- ☐ Cranky
- ☐ Cuddly
- ☐ Friendly
- ☐ Fussy
- ☐ Grumpy
- ☐ Happy
- ☐ Playful
- ☐ Quiet
- ☐ Sad
- ☐ Sick
- ☐ Sleepy
- ☐ Other: _____

NOTES FROM PARENT(S):
_____
_____
_____
_____
_____

WOKE UP AT:
A.M.
P.M.

LAST FED AT:
A.M.
P.M.

MEALS:

	TIME
Breakfast	
Snack	
Lunch	
Snack	
Dinner	

POTTY:

Time	Diaper	Potty	Dry	Wet	BM
____	☐	☐	☐	☐	☐
____	☐	☐	☐	☐	☐
____	☐	☐	☐	☐	☐
____	☐	☐	☐	☐	☐
____	☐	☐	☐	☐	☐
____	☐	☐	☐	☐	☐
____	☐	☐	☐	☐	☐

ACTIVITIES:
- ☐ FREE PLAY
- ☐ READING
- ☐ ARTS/CRAFTS
- ☐ MUSIC/SINGING
- ☐ OUTDOORS PLAY
- ☐ TV/MOVIE
- ☐ FIELD TRIP
- ☐ PLAYDATE WITH _____
- ☐ OTHER _____

SLEEP:

FROM	TO

ACCIDENT REPORT:

ACCIDENT	CARE GIVEN

MEDICATION(S):

TIME	TYPE	AMOUNT

SUPPLIES NEEDED:
_____
_____
_____
_____
_____

NOTES TO PARENTS:
_____
_____
_____
_____
_____

TIME IN: **TIME OUT:**

TODDLER REPORT

CHILD'S NAME:

DATE:

Ⓢ Ⓜ Ⓣ Ⓦ Ⓣ Ⓕ Ⓢ

MOOD:
- ☐ Chatty
- ☐ Happy
- ☐ Cranky
- ☐ Playful
- ☐ Cuddly
- ☐ Quiet
- ☐ Friendly
- ☐ Sad
- ☐ Fussy
- ☐ Sick
- ☐ Grumpy
- ☐ Sleepy
- ☐ Other: _____

NOTES FROM PARENT(S):

WOKE UP AT:
A.M.
P.M.

LAST FED AT:
A.M.
P.M.

MEALS:
	TIME
Breakfast	
Snack	
Lunch	
Snack	
Dinner	

POTTY:
Time	Diaper	Potty	Dry	Wet	BM
	☐	☐	☐	☐	☐
	☐	☐	☐	☐	☐
	☐	☐	☐	☐	☐
	☐	☐	☐	☐	☐
	☐	☐	☐	☐	☐
	☐	☐	☐	☐	☐
	☐	☐	☐	☐	☐

ACTIVITIES:
- ☐ FREE PLAY
- ☐ READING
- ☐ ARTS/CRAFTS
- ☐ MUSIC/SINGING
- ☐ OUTDOORS PLAY
- ☐ TV/MOVIE
- ☐ FIELD TRIP
- ☐ PLAYDATE WITH _____
- ☐ OTHER _____

SLEEP:
FROM	TO

ACCIDENT REPORT:
ACCIDENT	CARE GIVEN

MEDICATION(S):
TIME	TYPE	AMOUNT

SUPPLIES NEEDED:

NOTES TO PARENTS:

TIME IN: TIME OUT:

TODDLER REPORT

CHILD'S NAME:

DATE:

Ⓢ Ⓜ Ⓣ Ⓦ Ⓣ Ⓕ Ⓢ

MOOD:
- ☐ Chatty
- ☐ Happy
- ☐ Cranky
- ☐ Playful
- ☐ Cuddly
- ☐ Quiet
- ☐ Friendly
- ☐ Sad
- ☐ Fussy
- ☐ Sick
- ☐ Grumpy
- ☐ Sleepy
- ☐ Other: _____

NOTES FROM PARENT(S):
_____
_____
_____
_____
_____

WOKE UP AT:
A.M.
P.M.

LAST FED AT:
A.M.
P.M.

MEALS:

	TIME
Breakfast	
Snack	
Lunch	
Snack	
Dinner	

POTTY:

Time	Diaper	Potty	Dry	Wet	BM
____	☐	☐	☐	☐	☐
____	☐	☐	☐	☐	☐
____	☐	☐	☐	☐	☐
____	☐	☐	☐	☐	☐
____	☐	☐	☐	☐	☐
____	☐	☐	☐	☐	☐
____	☐	☐	☐	☐	☐

ACTIVITIES:
- ☐ FREE PLAY
- ☐ READING
- ☐ ARTS/CRAFTS
- ☐ MUSIC/SINGING
- ☐ OUTDOORS PLAY
- ☐ TV/MOVIE
- ☐ FIELD TRIP
- ☐ PLAYDATE WITH _____
- ☐ OTHER _____

SLEEP:

FROM	TO

ACCIDENT REPORT:

ACCIDENT	CARE GIVEN

MEDICATION(S):

TIME	TYPE	AMOUNT

SUPPLIES NEEDED:
_____
_____
_____
_____
_____

NOTES TO PARENTS:
_____
_____
_____
_____

TIME IN: **TIME OUT:**

TODDLER REPORT

CHILD'S NAME:

DATE:

Ⓢ Ⓜ Ⓣ Ⓦ Ⓣ Ⓕ Ⓢ

MOOD:
- ☐ Chatty
- ☐ Happy
- ☐ Cranky
- ☐ Playful
- ☐ Cuddly
- ☐ Quiet
- ☐ Friendly
- ☐ Sad
- ☐ Fussy
- ☐ Sick
- ☐ Grumpy
- ☐ Sleepy
- ☐ Other: _____

NOTES FROM PARENT(S):
_____
_____
_____
_____

WOKE UP AT:
A.M.
P.M.

LAST FED AT:
A.M.
P.M.

MEALS:
	TIME
Breakfast	
Snack	
Lunch	
Snack	
Dinner	

POTTY:
Time	Diaper	Potty	Dry	Wet	BM
___	☐	☐	☐	☐	☐
___	☐	☐	☐	☐	☐
___	☐	☐	☐	☐	☐
___	☐	☐	☐	☐	☐
___	☐	☐	☐	☐	☐
___	☐	☐	☐	☐	☐
___	☐	☐	☐	☐	☐

ACTIVITIES:
- ☐ FREE PLAY
- ☐ READING
- ☐ ARTS/CRAFTS
- ☐ MUSIC/SINGING
- ☐ OUTDOORS PLAY
- ☐ TV/MOVIE
- ☐ FIELD TRIP
- ☐ PLAYDATE WITH _____
- ☐ OTHER _____

SLEEP:
FROM	TO

ACCIDENT REPORT:
ACCIDENT	CARE GIVEN

MEDICATION(S):
TIME	TYPE	AMOUNT

SUPPLIES NEEDED:
_____
_____
_____
_____

NOTES TO PARENTS:
_____
_____
_____
_____
_____

TIME IN: **TIME OUT:**

TODDLER REPORT

CHILD'S NAME:

DATE:

Ⓢ Ⓜ Ⓣ Ⓦ Ⓣ Ⓕ Ⓢ

MOOD:
- ☐ Chatty
- ☐ Happy
- ☐ Cranky
- ☐ Playful
- ☐ Cuddly
- ☐ Quiet
- ☐ Friendly
- ☐ Sad
- ☐ Fussy
- ☐ Sick
- ☐ Grumpy
- ☐ Sleepy
- ☐ Other: _____

NOTES FROM PARENT(S):

WOKE UP AT:
A.M.
P.M.

LAST FED AT:
A.M.
P.M.

MEALS:

	TIME
Breakfast	
Snack	
Lunch	
Snack	
Dinner	

POTTY:

Time	Diaper	Potty	Dry	Wet	BM
	☐	☐	☐	☐	☐
	☐	☐	☐	☐	☐
	☐	☐	☐	☐	☐
	☐	☐	☐	☐	☐
	☐	☐	☐	☐	☐
	☐	☐	☐	☐	☐
	☐	☐	☐	☐	☐

ACTIVITIES:
- ☐ FREE PLAY
- ☐ READING
- ☐ ARTS/CRAFTS
- ☐ MUSIC/SINGING
- ☐ OUTDOORS PLAY
- ☐ TV/MOVIE
- ☐ FIELD TRIP
- ☐ PLAYDATE WITH _____
- ☐ OTHER _____

SLEEP:

FROM	TO

ACCIDENT REPORT:

ACCIDENT	CARE GIVEN

MEDICATION(S):

TIME	TYPE	AMOUNT

SUPPLIES NEEDED:

NOTES TO PARENTS:

TIME IN: TIME OUT:

TODDLER REPORT

CHILD'S NAME:

DATE:

Ⓢ Ⓜ Ⓣ Ⓦ Ⓣ Ⓕ Ⓢ

MOOD:
- ☐ Chatty
- ☐ Happy
- ☐ Cranky
- ☐ Playful
- ☐ Cuddly
- ☐ Quiet
- ☐ Friendly
- ☐ Sad
- ☐ Fussy
- ☐ Sick
- ☐ Grumpy
- ☐ Sleepy
- ☐ Other: _____

NOTES FROM PARENT(S):

WOKE UP AT:
A.M.
P.M.

LAST FED AT:
A.M.
P.M.

MEALS:

	TIME
Breakfast	
Snack	
Lunch	
Snack	
Dinner	

POTTY:

Time	Diaper	Potty	Dry	Wet	BM
___	☐	☐	☐	☐	☐
___	☐	☐	☐	☐	☐
___	☐	☐	☐	☐	☐
___	☐	☐	☐	☐	☐
___	☐	☐	☐	☐	☐
___	☐	☐	☐	☐	☐
___	☐	☐	☐	☐	☐

ACTIVITIES:
- ☐ FREE PLAY
- ☐ READING
- ☐ ARTS/CRAFTS
- ☐ MUSIC/SINGING
- ☐ OUTDOORS PLAY
- ☐ TV/MOVIE
- ☐ FIELD TRIP
- ☐ PLAYDATE WITH _____
- ☐ OTHER _____

SLEEP:

FROM	TO

ACCIDENT REPORT:

ACCIDENT	CARE GIVEN

MEDICATION(S):

TIME	TYPE	AMOUNT

SUPPLIES NEEDED:

NOTES TO PARENTS:

TIME IN: **TIME OUT:**

TODDLER REPORT

CHILD'S NAME: _____

DATE: _____

Ⓢ Ⓜ Ⓣ Ⓦ Ⓣ Ⓕ Ⓢ

MOOD:
- ☐ Chatty
- ☐ Happy
- ☐ Cranky
- ☐ Playful
- ☐ Cuddly
- ☐ Quiet
- ☐ Friendly
- ☐ Sad
- ☐ Fussy
- ☐ Sick
- ☐ Grumpy
- ☐ Sleepy
- ☐ Other: _____

NOTES FROM PARENT(S):
_____
_____
_____
_____
_____

WOKE UP AT:
_____ A.M. / P.M.

LAST FED AT:
_____ A.M. / P.M.

MEALS:

	TIME
Breakfast	
Snack	
Lunch	
Snack	
Dinner	

POTTY:

Time	Diaper	Potty	Dry	Wet	BM
_____	☐	☐	☐	☐	☐
_____	☐	☐	☐	☐	☐
_____	☐	☐	☐	☐	☐
_____	☐	☐	☐	☐	☐
_____	☐	☐	☐	☐	☐
_____	☐	☐	☐	☐	☐
_____	☐	☐	☐	☐	☐

ACTIVITIES:
- ☐ FREE PLAY
- ☐ READING
- ☐ ARTS/CRAFTS
- ☐ MUSIC/SINGING
- ☐ OUTDOORS PLAY
- ☐ TV/MOVIE
- ☐ FIELD TRIP
- ☐ PLAYDATE WITH _____
- ☐ OTHER _____

SLEEP:

FROM	TO

ACCIDENT REPORT:

ACCIDENT	CARE GIVEN

MEDICATION(S):

TIME	TYPE	AMOUNT

SUPPLIES NEEDED:
_____
_____
_____
_____
_____

NOTES TO PARENTS:
_____
_____
_____
_____
_____

TIME IN: _____ **TIME OUT:** _____

TODDLER REPORT

CHILD'S NAME:

DATE:

Ⓢ Ⓜ Ⓣ Ⓦ Ⓣ Ⓕ Ⓢ

MOOD:
- ☐ Chatty
- ☐ Happy
- ☐ Cranky
- ☐ Playful
- ☐ Cuddly
- ☐ Quiet
- ☐ Friendly
- ☐ Sad
- ☐ Fussy
- ☐ Sick
- ☐ Grumpy
- ☐ Sleepy
- ☐ Other: _____

NOTES FROM PARENT(S):
_____
_____
_____
_____

WOKE UP AT:
A.M.
P.M.

LAST FED AT:
A.M.
P.M.

MEALS:
	TIME
Breakfast	
Snack	
Lunch	
Snack	
Dinner	

POTTY:
Time	Diaper	Potty	Dry	Wet	BM
____	☐	☐	☐	☐	☐
____	☐	☐	☐	☐	☐
____	☐	☐	☐	☐	☐
____	☐	☐	☐	☐	☐
____	☐	☐	☐	☐	☐
____	☐	☐	☐	☐	☐
____	☐	☐	☐	☐	☐

ACTIVITIES:
- ☐ FREE PLAY
- ☐ READING
- ☐ ARTS/CRAFTS
- ☐ MUSIC/SINGING
- ☐ OUTDOORS PLAY
- ☐ TV/MOVIE
- ☐ FIELD TRIP
- ☐ PLAYDATE WITH _____
- ☐ OTHER _____

SLEEP:
FROM	TO

ACCIDENT REPORT:
ACCIDENT	CARE GIVEN

MEDICATION(S):
TIME	TYPE	AMOUNT

SUPPLIES NEEDED:
_____
_____
_____
_____
_____

NOTES TO PARENTS:
_____
_____
_____
_____
_____

TIME IN: **TIME OUT:**

TODDLER REPORT

CHILD'S NAME:

DATE:

Ⓢ Ⓜ Ⓣ Ⓦ Ⓣ Ⓕ Ⓢ

MOOD:
- ☐ Chatty
- ☐ Happy
- ☐ Cranky
- ☐ Playful
- ☐ Cuddly
- ☐ Quiet
- ☐ Friendly
- ☐ Sad
- ☐ Fussy
- ☐ Sick
- ☐ Grumpy
- ☐ Sleepy
- ☐ Other: _____

NOTES FROM PARENT(S):

WOKE UP AT:
A.M.
P.M.

LAST FED AT:
A.M.
P.M.

MEALS:

	TIME
Breakfast	
Snack	
Lunch	
Snack	
Dinner	

POTTY:

Time	Diaper	Potty	Dry	Wet	BM
	☐	☐	☐	☐	☐
	☐	☐	☐	☐	☐
	☐	☐	☐	☐	☐
	☐	☐	☐	☐	☐
	☐	☐	☐	☐	☐
	☐	☐	☐	☐	☐
	☐	☐	☐	☐	☐

ACTIVITIES:
- ☐ FREE PLAY
- ☐ READING
- ☐ ARTS/CRAFTS
- ☐ MUSIC/SINGING
- ☐ OUTDOORS PLAY
- ☐ TV/MOVIE
- ☐ FIELD TRIP
- ☐ PLAYDATE WITH _____
- ☐ OTHER _____

SLEEP:

FROM	TO

ACCIDENT REPORT:

ACCIDENT	CARE GIVEN

MEDICATION(S):

TIME	TYPE	AMOUNT

SUPPLIES NEEDED:

NOTES TO PARENTS:

TIME IN: **TIME OUT:**

TODDLER REPORT

CHILD'S NAME:

DATE:

(S) (M) (T) (W) (T) (F) (S)

MOOD:
- ☐ Chatty
- ☐ Happy
- ☐ Cranky
- ☐ Playful
- ☐ Cuddly
- ☐ Quiet
- ☐ Friendly
- ☐ Sad
- ☐ Fussy
- ☐ Sick
- ☐ Grumpy
- ☐ Sleepy
- ☐ Other: _____

NOTES FROM PARENT(S):
_____
_____
_____
_____

WOKE UP AT:
A.M.
P.M.

LAST FED AT:
A.M.
P.M.

MEALS:
	TIME
Breakfast	
Snack	
Lunch	
Snack	
Dinner	

POTTY:
Time	Diaper	Potty	Dry	Wet	BM
	☐	☐	☐	☐	☐
	☐	☐	☐	☐	☐
	☐	☐	☐	☐	☐
	☐	☐	☐	☐	☐
	☐	☐	☐	☐	☐
	☐	☐	☐	☐	☐
	☐	☐	☐	☐	☐

ACTIVITIES:
- ☐ FREE PLAY
- ☐ READING
- ☐ ARTS/CRAFTS
- ☐ MUSIC/SINGING
- ☐ OUTDOORS PLAY
- ☐ TV/MOVIE
- ☐ FIELD TRIP
- ☐ PLAYDATE WITH _____
- ☐ OTHER _____

SLEEP:
FROM	TO

ACCIDENT REPORT:
ACCIDENT	CARE GIVEN

MEDICATION(S):
TIME	TYPE	AMOUNT

SUPPLIES NEEDED:
_____
_____
_____
_____
_____

NOTES TO PARENTS:
_____
_____
_____
_____
_____

TIME IN: TIME OUT:

TODDLER REPORT

CHILD'S NAME:

DATE:

Ⓢ Ⓜ Ⓣ Ⓦ Ⓣ Ⓕ Ⓢ

MOOD:
- ☐ Chatty
- ☐ Cranky
- ☐ Cuddly
- ☐ Friendly
- ☐ Fussy
- ☐ Grumpy
- ☐ Happy
- ☐ Playful
- ☐ Quiet
- ☐ Sad
- ☐ Sick
- ☐ Sleepy
- ☐ Other: _____

NOTES FROM PARENT(S):
_____
_____
_____
_____
_____

WOKE UP AT:
A.M.
P.M.

LAST FED AT:
A.M.
P.M.

MEALS:

	TIME
Breakfast	
Snack	
Lunch	
Snack	
Dinner	

POTTY:

Time	Diaper	Potty	Dry	Wet	BM
	☐	☐	☐	☐	☐
	☐	☐	☐	☐	☐
	☐	☐	☐	☐	☐
	☐	☐	☐	☐	☐
	☐	☐	☐	☐	☐
	☐	☐	☐	☐	☐
	☐	☐	☐	☐	☐

ACTIVITIES:
- ☐ FREE PLAY
- ☐ READING
- ☐ ARTS/CRAFTS
- ☐ MUSIC/SINGING
- ☐ OUTDOORS PLAY
- ☐ TV/MOVIE
- ☐ FIELD TRIP
- ☐ PLAYDATE WITH _____
- ☐ OTHER _____

SLEEP:

FROM	TO

ACCIDENT REPORT:

ACCIDENT	CARE GIVEN

MEDICATION(S):

TIME	TYPE	AMOUNT

SUPPLIES NEEDED:
_____
_____
_____
_____
_____

NOTES TO PARENTS:
_____
_____
_____
_____

TIME IN: **TIME OUT:**

TODDLER REPORT

DATE:

CHILD'S NAME:

(S) (M) (T) (W) (T) (F) (S)

MOOD:
- ☐ Chatty
- ☐ Happy
- ☐ Cranky
- ☐ Playful
- ☐ Cuddly
- ☐ Quiet
- ☐ Friendly
- ☐ Sad
- ☐ Fussy
- ☐ Sick
- ☐ Grumpy
- ☐ Sleepy
- ☐ Other: _____

NOTES FROM PARENT(S):

WOKE UP AT:
A.M.
P.M.

LAST FED AT:
A.M.
P.M.

MEALS:

	TIME
Breakfast	
Snack	
Lunch	
Snack	
Dinner	

POTTY:

Time	Diaper	Potty	Dry	Wet	BM
	☐	☐	☐	☐	☐
	☐	☐	☐	☐	☐
	☐	☐	☐	☐	☐
	☐	☐	☐	☐	☐
	☐	☐	☐	☐	☐
	☐	☐	☐	☐	☐
	☐	☐	☐	☐	☐

ACTIVITIES:
- ☐ FREE PLAY
- ☐ READING
- ☐ ARTS/CRAFTS
- ☐ MUSIC/SINGING
- ☐ OUTDOORS PLAY
- ☐ TV/MOVIE
- ☐ FIELD TRIP
- ☐ PLAYDATE WITH _____
- ☐ OTHER _____

SLEEP:

FROM	TO

ACCIDENT REPORT:

ACCIDENT	CARE GIVEN

MEDICATION(S):

TIME	TYPE	AMOUNT

SUPPLIES NEEDED:

NOTES TO PARENTS:

TIME IN: **TIME OUT:**

TODDLER REPORT

CHILD'S NAME:

DATE:

Ⓢ Ⓜ Ⓣ Ⓦ Ⓣ Ⓕ Ⓢ

MOOD:
- ☐ Chatty
- ☐ Happy
- ☐ Cranky
- ☐ Playful
- ☐ Cuddly
- ☐ Quiet
- ☐ Friendly
- ☐ Sad
- ☐ Fussy
- ☐ Sick
- ☐ Grumpy
- ☐ Sleepy
- ☐ Other: _____

NOTES FROM PARENT(S):
_____
_____
_____
_____
_____

WOKE UP AT:
A.M.
P.M.

LAST FED AT:
A.M.
P.M.

MEALS:

	TIME
Breakfast	
Snack	
Lunch	
Snack	
Dinner	

POTTY:

Time	Diaper	Potty	Dry	Wet	BM
_____	☐	☐	☐	☐	☐
_____	☐	☐	☐	☐	☐
_____	☐	☐	☐	☐	☐
_____	☐	☐	☐	☐	☐
_____	☐	☐	☐	☐	☐
_____	☐	☐	☐	☐	☐
_____	☐	☐	☐	☐	☐

ACTIVITIES:
- ☐ FREE PLAY
- ☐ READING
- ☐ ARTS/CRAFTS
- ☐ MUSIC/SINGING
- ☐ OUTDOORS PLAY
- ☐ TV/MOVIE
- ☐ FIELD TRIP
- ☐ PLAYDATE WITH _____
- ☐ OTHER _____

SLEEP:

FROM	TO

ACCIDENT REPORT:

ACCIDENT	CARE GIVEN

MEDICATION(S):

TIME	TYPE	AMOUNT

SUPPLIES NEEDED:
_____
_____
_____
_____
_____

NOTES TO PARENTS:
_____
_____
_____
_____
_____
_____

TIME IN: **TIME OUT:**

TODDLER REPORT

CHILD'S NAME:

DATE:

Ⓢ Ⓜ Ⓣ Ⓦ Ⓣ Ⓕ Ⓢ

MOOD:
- ☐ Chatty
- ☐ Happy
- ☐ Cranky
- ☐ Playful
- ☐ Cuddly
- ☐ Quiet
- ☐ Friendly
- ☐ Sad
- ☐ Fussy
- ☐ Sick
- ☐ Grumpy
- ☐ Sleepy
- ☐ Other: _____

NOTES FROM PARENT(S):
_____
_____
_____
_____
_____

WOKE UP AT:
A.M.
P.M.

LAST FED AT:
A.M.
P.M.

MEALS:

	TIME
Breakfast	
Snack	
Lunch	
Snack	
Dinner	

POTTY:

Time	Diaper	Potty	Dry	Wet	BM
___	☐	☐	☐	☐	☐
___	☐	☐	☐	☐	☐
___	☐	☐	☐	☐	☐
___	☐	☐	☐	☐	☐
___	☐	☐	☐	☐	☐
___	☐	☐	☐	☐	☐
___	☐	☐	☐	☐	☐

ACTIVITIES:
- ☐ FREE PLAY
- ☐ READING
- ☐ ARTS/CRAFTS
- ☐ MUSIC/SINGING
- ☐ OUTDOORS PLAY
- ☐ TV/MOVIE
- ☐ FIELD TRIP
- ☐ PLAYDATE WITH _____
- ☐ OTHER _____

SLEEP:

FROM	TO

ACCIDENT REPORT:

ACCIDENT	CARE GIVEN

MEDICATION(S):

TIME	TYPE	AMOUNT

SUPPLIES NEEDED:
_____
_____
_____
_____
_____

NOTES TO PARENTS:
_____
_____
_____
_____
_____

TIME IN: TIME OUT:

TODDLER REPORT

DATE: _____

CHILD'S NAME: _____

Ⓢ Ⓜ Ⓣ Ⓦ Ⓣ Ⓕ Ⓢ

MOOD:
- ☐ Chatty
- ☐ Happy
- ☐ Cranky
- ☐ Playful
- ☐ Cuddly
- ☐ Quiet
- ☐ Friendly
- ☐ Sad
- ☐ Fussy
- ☐ Sick
- ☐ Grumpy
- ☐ Sleepy
- ☐ Other: _____

NOTES FROM PARENT(S):
_____
_____
_____
_____
_____

WOKE UP AT:
_____ A.M. / P.M.

LAST FED AT:
_____ A.M. / P.M.

MEALS:

	TIME
Breakfast	
Snack	
Lunch	
Snack	
Dinner	

POTTY:

Time	Diaper	Potty	Dry	Wet	BM
___	☐	☐	☐	☐	☐
___	☐	☐	☐	☐	☐
___	☐	☐	☐	☐	☐
___	☐	☐	☐	☐	☐
___	☐	☐	☐	☐	☐
___	☐	☐	☐	☐	☐
___	☐	☐	☐	☐	☐

ACTIVITIES:
- ☐ FREE PLAY
- ☐ READING
- ☐ ARTS/CRAFTS
- ☐ MUSIC/SINGING
- ☐ OUTDOORS PLAY
- ☐ TV/MOVIE
- ☐ FIELD TRIP
- ☐ PLAYDATE WITH _____
- ☐ OTHER _____

SLEEP:

FROM	TO

ACCIDENT REPORT:

ACCIDENT	CARE GIVEN

MEDICATION(S):

TIME	TYPE	AMOUNT

SUPPLIES NEEDED:
_____
_____
_____
_____
_____

NOTES TO PARENTS:
_____
_____
_____
_____
_____

TIME IN: _____   TIME OUT: _____

TODDLER REPORT

CHILD'S NAME:

DATE:

Ⓢ Ⓜ Ⓣ Ⓦ Ⓣ Ⓕ Ⓢ

MOOD:
- ☐ Chatty
- ☐ Happy
- ☐ Cranky
- ☐ Playful
- ☐ Cuddly
- ☐ Quiet
- ☐ Friendly
- ☐ Sad
- ☐ Fussy
- ☐ Sick
- ☐ Grumpy
- ☐ Sleepy
- ☐ Other: _____

NOTES FROM PARENT(S):

WOKE UP AT:
A.M.
P.M.

LAST FED AT:
A.M.
P.M.

MEALS:

	TIME
Breakfast	
Snack	
Lunch	
Snack	
Dinner	

POTTY:

Time	Diaper	Potty	Dry	Wet	BM
	☐	☐	☐	☐	☐
	☐	☐	☐	☐	☐
	☐	☐	☐	☐	☐
	☐	☐	☐	☐	☐
	☐	☐	☐	☐	☐
	☐	☐	☐	☐	☐
	☐	☐	☐	☐	☐

ACTIVITIES:
- ☐ FREE PLAY
- ☐ READING
- ☐ ARTS/CRAFTS
- ☐ MUSIC/SINGING
- ☐ OUTDOORS PLAY
- ☐ TV/MOVIE
- ☐ FIELD TRIP
- ☐ PLAYDATE WITH _____
- ☐ OTHER _____

SLEEP:

FROM	TO

ACCIDENT REPORT:

ACCIDENT	CARE GIVEN

MEDICATION(S):

TIME	TYPE	AMOUNT

SUPPLIES NEEDED:

NOTES TO PARENTS:

TIME IN: **TIME OUT:**

TODDLER REPORT

CHILD'S NAME:

DATE:

Ⓢ Ⓜ Ⓣ Ⓦ Ⓣ Ⓕ Ⓢ

MOOD:
- ☐ Chatty
- ☐ Happy
- ☐ Cranky
- ☐ Playful
- ☐ Cuddly
- ☐ Quiet
- ☐ Friendly
- ☐ Sad
- ☐ Fussy
- ☐ Sick
- ☐ Grumpy
- ☐ Sleepy
- ☐ Other: _____

NOTES FROM PARENT(S):

WOKE UP AT:
A.M.
P.M.

LAST FED AT:
A.M.
P.M.

MEALS:

	TIME
Breakfast	
Snack	
Lunch	
Snack	
Dinner	

POTTY:

Time	Diaper	Potty	Dry	Wet	BM
___	☐	☐	☐	☐	☐
___	☐	☐	☐	☐	☐
___	☐	☐	☐	☐	☐
___	☐	☐	☐	☐	☐
___	☐	☐	☐	☐	☐
___	☐	☐	☐	☐	☐
___	☐	☐	☐	☐	☐

ACTIVITIES:
- ☐ FREE PLAY
- ☐ READING
- ☐ ARTS/CRAFTS
- ☐ MUSIC/SINGING
- ☐ OUTDOORS PLAY
- ☐ TV/MOVIE
- ☐ FIELD TRIP
- ☐ PLAYDATE WITH _____
- ☐ OTHER _____

SLEEP:
FROM	TO

ACCIDENT REPORT:
ACCIDENT	CARE GIVEN

MEDICATION(S):
TIME	TYPE	AMOUNT

SUPPLIES NEEDED:

NOTES TO PARENTS:

TIME IN: TIME OUT:

TODDLER REPORT

CHILD'S NAME:

DATE:

Ⓢ Ⓜ Ⓣ Ⓦ Ⓣ Ⓕ Ⓢ

MOOD:
- ☐ Chatty
- ☐ Happy
- ☐ Cranky
- ☐ Playful
- ☐ Cuddly
- ☐ Quiet
- ☐ Friendly
- ☐ Sad
- ☐ Fussy
- ☐ Sick
- ☐ Grumpy
- ☐ Sleepy
- ☐ Other: _____

NOTES FROM PARENT(S):
_____
_____
_____
_____
_____

WOKE UP AT:
A.M.
P.M.

LAST FED AT:
A.M.
P.M.

MEALS:

	TIME
Breakfast	
Snack	
Lunch	
Snack	
Dinner	

POTTY:

Time	Diaper	Potty	Dry	Wet	BM
____	☐	☐	☐	☐	☐
____	☐	☐	☐	☐	☐
____	☐	☐	☐	☐	☐
____	☐	☐	☐	☐	☐
____	☐	☐	☐	☐	☐
____	☐	☐	☐	☐	☐
____	☐	☐	☐	☐	☐

ACTIVITIES:
- ☐ FREE PLAY
- ☐ READING
- ☐ ARTS/CRAFTS
- ☐ MUSIC/SINGING
- ☐ OUTDOORS PLAY
- ☐ TV/MOVIE
- ☐ FIELD TRIP
- ☐ PLAYDATE WITH _____
- ☐ OTHER _____

SLEEP:

FROM	TO

ACCIDENT REPORT:

ACCIDENT	CARE GIVEN

MEDICATION(S):

TIME	TYPE	AMOUNT

SUPPLIES NEEDED:
_____
_____
_____
_____
_____

NOTES TO PARENTS:
_____
_____
_____
_____
_____

TIME IN: **TIME OUT:**

TODDLER REPORT

DATE: _____

CHILD'S NAME: _____

(S) (M) (T) (W) (T) (F) (S)

MOOD:
- ☐ Chatty
- ☐ Happy
- ☐ Cranky
- ☐ Playful
- ☐ Cuddly
- ☐ Quiet
- ☐ Friendly
- ☐ Sad
- ☐ Fussy
- ☐ Sick
- ☐ Grumpy
- ☐ Sleepy
- ☐ Other: _____

NOTES FROM PARENT(S):
_____
_____
_____
_____

WOKE UP AT:
_____
A.M.
P.M.

LAST FED AT:
_____
A.M.
P.M.

MEALS:

	TIME
Breakfast	
Snack	
Lunch	
Snack	
Dinner	

POTTY:

Time	Diaper	Potty	Dry	Wet	BM
	☐	☐	☐	☐	☐
	☐	☐	☐	☐	☐
	☐	☐	☐	☐	☐
	☐	☐	☐	☐	☐
	☐	☐	☐	☐	☐
	☐	☐	☐	☐	☐
	☐	☐	☐	☐	☐

ACTIVITIES:
- ☐ FREE PLAY
- ☐ READING
- ☐ ARTS/CRAFTS
- ☐ MUSIC/SINGING
- ☐ OUTDOORS PLAY
- ☐ TV/MOVIE
- ☐ FIELD TRIP
- ☐ PLAYDATE WITH _____
- ☐ OTHER _____

SLEEP:

FROM	TO

ACCIDENT REPORT:

ACCIDENT	CARE GIVEN

MEDICATION(S):

TIME	TYPE	AMOUNT

SUPPLIES NEEDED:
_____
_____
_____
_____
_____

NOTES TO PARENTS:
_____
_____
_____
_____
_____

TIME IN: _____ TIME OUT: _____

TODDLER REPORT

CHILD'S NAME:

DATE:

S M T W T F S

MOOD:
- ☐ Chatty
- ☐ Happy
- ☐ Cranky
- ☐ Playful
- ☐ Cuddly
- ☐ Quiet
- ☐ Friendly
- ☐ Sad
- ☐ Fussy
- ☐ Sick
- ☐ Grumpy
- ☐ Sleepy
- ☐ Other: _____

NOTES FROM PARENT(S):
_____
_____
_____
_____
_____

WOKE UP AT:
A.M.
P.M.

LAST FED AT:
A.M.
P.M.

MEALS:

	TIME
Breakfast	
Snack	
Lunch	
Snack	
Dinner	

POTTY:

Time	Diaper	Potty	Dry	Wet	BM
_____	☐	☐	☐	☐	☐
_____	☐	☐	☐	☐	☐
_____	☐	☐	☐	☐	☐
_____	☐	☐	☐	☐	☐
_____	☐	☐	☐	☐	☐
_____	☐	☐	☐	☐	☐
_____	☐	☐	☐	☐	☐

ACTIVITIES:
- ☐ FREE PLAY
- ☐ READING
- ☐ ARTS/CRAFTS
- ☐ MUSIC/SINGING
- ☐ OUTDOORS PLAY
- ☐ TV/MOVIE
- ☐ FIELD TRIP
- ☐ PLAYDATE WITH _____
- ☐ OTHER _____

SLEEP:

FROM	TO

ACCIDENT REPORT:

ACCIDENT	CARE GIVEN

MEDICATION(S):

TIME	TYPE	AMOUNT

SUPPLIES NEEDED:
_____
_____
_____
_____
_____
_____

NOTES TO PARENTS:
_____
_____
_____
_____
_____

TIME IN: **TIME OUT:**

TODDLER REPORT

CHILD'S NAME:

DATE:

Ⓢ Ⓜ Ⓣ Ⓦ Ⓣ Ⓕ Ⓢ

MOOD:
- ☐ Chatty
- ☐ Happy
- ☐ Cranky
- ☐ Playful
- ☐ Cuddly
- ☐ Quiet
- ☐ Friendly
- ☐ Sad
- ☐ Fussy
- ☐ Sick
- ☐ Grumpy
- ☐ Sleepy
- ☐ Other: _____

NOTES FROM PARENT(S):
_____
_____
_____
_____

WOKE UP AT:
A.M.
P.M.

LAST FED AT:
A.M.
P.M.

MEALS:

	TIME
Breakfast	
Snack	
Lunch	
Snack	
Dinner	

POTTY:

Time	Diaper	Potty	Dry	Wet	BM
____	☐	☐	☐	☐	☐
____	☐	☐	☐	☐	☐
____	☐	☐	☐	☐	☐
____	☐	☐	☐	☐	☐
____	☐	☐	☐	☐	☐
____	☐	☐	☐	☐	☐
____	☐	☐	☐	☐	☐

ACTIVITIES:
- ☐ FREE PLAY
- ☐ READING
- ☐ ARTS/CRAFTS
- ☐ MUSIC/SINGING
- ☐ OUTDOORS PLAY
- ☐ TV/MOVIE
- ☐ FIELD TRIP
- ☐ PLAYDATE WITH _____
- ☐ OTHER _____

SLEEP:

FROM	TO

ACCIDENT REPORT:

ACCIDENT	CARE GIVEN

MEDICATION(S):

TIME	TYPE	AMOUNT

SUPPLIES NEEDED:
_____
_____
_____
_____
_____

NOTES TO PARENTS:
_____
_____
_____
_____

TIME IN: **TIME OUT:**

TODDLER REPORT

CHILD'S NAME:

DATE:

Ⓢ Ⓜ Ⓣ Ⓦ Ⓣ Ⓕ Ⓢ

MOOD:
- ☐ Chatty
- ☐ Happy
- ☐ Cranky
- ☐ Playful
- ☐ Cuddly
- ☐ Quiet
- ☐ Friendly
- ☐ Sad
- ☐ Fussy
- ☐ Sick
- ☐ Grumpy
- ☐ Sleepy
- ☐ Other: _____

NOTES FROM PARENT(S):
_____
_____
_____
_____
_____

WOKE UP AT:
A.M.
P.M.

LAST FED AT:
A.M.
P.M.

MEALS:

	TIME
Breakfast	
Snack	
Lunch	
Snack	
Dinner	

POTTY:

Time	Diaper	Potty	Dry	Wet	BM
____	☐	☐	☐	☐	☐
____	☐	☐	☐	☐	☐
____	☐	☐	☐	☐	☐
____	☐	☐	☐	☐	☐
____	☐	☐	☐	☐	☐
____	☐	☐	☐	☐	☐
____	☐	☐	☐	☐	☐

ACTIVITIES:
- ☐ FREE PLAY
- ☐ READING
- ☐ ARTS/CRAFTS
- ☐ MUSIC/SINGING
- ☐ OUTDOORS PLAY
- ☐ TV/MOVIE
- ☐ FIELD TRIP
- ☐ PLAYDATE WITH _____
- ☐ OTHER _____

SLEEP:

FROM	TO

ACCIDENT REPORT:

ACCIDENT	CARE GIVEN

MEDICATION(S):

TIME	TYPE	AMOUNT

SUPPLIES NEEDED:
_____
_____
_____
_____
_____

NOTES TO PARENTS:
_____
_____
_____
_____
_____
_____

TIME IN: **TIME OUT:**

TODDLER REPORT

DATE: _____

CHILD'S NAME: _____

(S) (M) (T) (W) (T) (F) (S)

MOOD:
- ☐ Chatty
- ☐ Happy
- ☐ Cranky
- ☐ Playful
- ☐ Cuddly
- ☐ Quiet
- ☐ Friendly
- ☐ Sad
- ☐ Fussy
- ☐ Sick
- ☐ Grumpy
- ☐ Sleepy
- ☐ Other: _____

NOTES FROM PARENT(S):
_____
_____
_____
_____
_____

WOKE UP AT:
A.M.
P.M.

LAST FED AT:
A.M.
P.M.

MEALS:

	TIME
Breakfast	
Snack	
Lunch	
Snack	
Dinner	

POTTY:

Time	Diaper	Potty	Dry	Wet	BM
___	☐	☐	☐	☐	☐
___	☐	☐	☐	☐	☐
___	☐	☐	☐	☐	☐
___	☐	☐	☐	☐	☐
___	☐	☐	☐	☐	☐
___	☐	☐	☐	☐	☐
___	☐	☐	☐	☐	☐

ACTIVITIES:
- ☐ FREE PLAY
- ☐ READING
- ☐ ARTS/CRAFTS
- ☐ MUSIC/SINGING
- ☐ OUTDOORS PLAY
- ☐ TV/MOVIE
- ☐ FIELD TRIP
- ☐ PLAYDATE WITH _____
- ☐ OTHER _____

SLEEP:

FROM	TO

ACCIDENT REPORT:

ACCIDENT	CARE GIVEN

MEDICATION(S):

TIME	TYPE	AMOUNT

SUPPLIES NEEDED:
_____
_____
_____
_____
_____

NOTES TO PARENTS:
_____
_____
_____
_____
_____

TIME IN: _____   **TIME OUT:** _____

TODDLER REPORT

CHILD'S NAME:

DATE:

Ⓢ Ⓜ Ⓣ Ⓦ Ⓣ Ⓕ Ⓢ

MOOD:
- ☐ Chatty
- ☐ Happy
- ☐ Cranky
- ☐ Playful
- ☐ Cuddly
- ☐ Quiet
- ☐ Friendly
- ☐ Sad
- ☐ Fussy
- ☐ Sick
- ☐ Grumpy
- ☐ Sleepy
- ☐ Other: _____

NOTES FROM PARENT(S):
_____
_____
_____
_____

WOKE UP AT:
A.M.
P.M.

LAST FED AT:
A.M.
P.M.

MEALS:
	TIME
Breakfast	
Snack	
Lunch	
Snack	
Dinner	

POTTY:
Time	Diaper	Potty	Dry	Wet	BM
___	☐	☐	☐	☐	☐
___	☐	☐	☐	☐	☐
___	☐	☐	☐	☐	☐
___	☐	☐	☐	☐	☐
___	☐	☐	☐	☐	☐
___	☐	☐	☐	☐	☐
___	☐	☐	☐	☐	☐

ACTIVITIES:
- ☐ FREE PLAY
- ☐ READING
- ☐ ARTS/CRAFTS
- ☐ MUSIC/SINGING
- ☐ OUTDOORS PLAY
- ☐ TV/MOVIE
- ☐ FIELD TRIP
- ☐ PLAYDATE WITH _____
- ☐ OTHER _____

SLEEP:
FROM	TO

ACCIDENT REPORT:
ACCIDENT	CARE GIVEN

MEDICATION(S):
TIME	TYPE	AMOUNT

SUPPLIES NEEDED:
_____
_____
_____
_____

NOTES TO PARENTS:
_____
_____
_____
_____
_____

TIME IN: **TIME OUT:**

TODDLER REPORT

DATE: _____

CHILD'S NAME: _____

(S) (M) (T) (W) (T) (F) (S)

MOOD:
- ☐ Chatty
- ☐ Happy
- ☐ Cranky
- ☐ Playful
- ☐ Cuddly
- ☐ Quiet
- ☐ Friendly
- ☐ Sad
- ☐ Fussy
- ☐ Sick
- ☐ Grumpy
- ☐ Sleepy
- ☐ Other: _____

NOTES FROM PARENT(S):
_____
_____
_____
_____
_____

WOKE UP AT:
_____
A.M.
P.M.

LAST FED AT:
_____
A.M.
P.M.

MEALS:

	TIME
Breakfast	
Snack	
Lunch	
Snack	
Dinner	

POTTY:

Time	Diaper	Potty	Dry	Wet	BM
____	☐	☐	☐	☐	☐
____	☐	☐	☐	☐	☐
____	☐	☐	☐	☐	☐
____	☐	☐	☐	☐	☐
____	☐	☐	☐	☐	☐
____	☐	☐	☐	☐	☐
____	☐	☐	☐	☐	☐

ACTIVITIES:
- ☐ FREE PLAY
- ☐ READING
- ☐ ARTS/CRAFTS
- ☐ MUSIC/SINGING
- ☐ OUTDOORS PLAY
- ☐ TV/MOVIE
- ☐ FIELD TRIP
- ☐ PLAYDATE WITH _____
- ☐ OTHER _____

SLEEP:

FROM	TO

ACCIDENT REPORT:

ACCIDENT	CARE GIVEN

MEDICATION(S):

TIME	TYPE	AMOUNT

SUPPLIES NEEDED:
_____
_____
_____
_____
_____

NOTES TO PARENTS:
_____
_____
_____
_____
_____

TIME IN: _____   TIME OUT: _____

TODDLER REPORT

DATE:

CHILD'S NAME:

Ⓢ Ⓜ Ⓣ Ⓦ Ⓣ Ⓕ Ⓢ

MOOD:
- ☐ Chatty
- ☐ Happy
- ☐ Cranky
- ☐ Playful
- ☐ Cuddly
- ☐ Quiet
- ☐ Friendly
- ☐ Sad
- ☐ Fussy
- ☐ Sick
- ☐ Grumpy
- ☐ Sleepy
- ☐ Other: _____

NOTES FROM PARENT(S):

WOKE UP AT:
A.M.
P.M.

LAST FED AT:
A.M.
P.M.

MEALS:
	TIME
Breakfast	
Snack	
Lunch	
Snack	
Dinner	

POTTY:
Time	Diaper	Potty	Dry	Wet	BM
	☐	☐	☐	☐	☐
	☐	☐	☐	☐	☐
	☐	☐	☐	☐	☐
	☐	☐	☐	☐	☐
	☐	☐	☐	☐	☐
	☐	☐	☐	☐	☐
	☐	☐	☐	☐	☐

ACTIVITIES:
- ☐ FREE PLAY
- ☐ READING
- ☐ ARTS/CRAFTS
- ☐ MUSIC/SINGING
- ☐ OUTDOORS PLAY
- ☐ TV/MOVIE
- ☐ FIELD TRIP
- ☐ PLAYDATE WITH _____
- ☐ OTHER _____

SLEEP:
FROM	TO

ACCIDENT REPORT:
ACCIDENT	CARE GIVEN

MEDICATION(S):
TIME	TYPE	AMOUNT

SUPPLIES NEEDED:

NOTES TO PARENTS:

TIME IN: **TIME OUT:**

TODDLER REPORT

CHILD'S NAME:

DATE:

Ⓢ Ⓜ Ⓣ Ⓦ Ⓣ Ⓕ Ⓢ

MOOD:
- ☐ Chatty
- ☐ Cranky
- ☐ Cuddly
- ☐ Friendly
- ☐ Fussy
- ☐ Grumpy
- ☐ Happy
- ☐ Playful
- ☐ Quiet
- ☐ Sad
- ☐ Sick
- ☐ Sleepy
- ☐ Other: _____

NOTES FROM PARENT(S):

WOKE UP AT:
A.M.
P.M.

LAST FED AT:
A.M.
P.M.

MEALS:

	TIME
Breakfast	
Snack	
Lunch	
Snack	
Dinner	

POTTY:

Time	Diaper	Potty	Dry	Wet	BM
	☐	☐	☐	☐	☐
	☐	☐	☐	☐	☐
	☐	☐	☐	☐	☐
	☐	☐	☐	☐	☐
	☐	☐	☐	☐	☐
	☐	☐	☐	☐	☐
	☐	☐	☐	☐	☐

ACTIVITIES:
- ☐ FREE PLAY
- ☐ READING
- ☐ ARTS/CRAFTS
- ☐ MUSIC/SINGING
- ☐ OUTDOORS PLAY
- ☐ TV/MOVIE
- ☐ FIELD TRIP
- ☐ PLAYDATE WITH _____
- ☐ OTHER _____

SLEEP:

FROM	TO

ACCIDENT REPORT:

ACCIDENT	CARE GIVEN

MEDICATION(S):

TIME	TYPE	AMOUNT

SUPPLIES NEEDED:

NOTES TO PARENTS:

TIME IN: **TIME OUT:**

TODDLER REPORT

CHILD'S NAME: _____

DATE: _____

Ⓢ Ⓜ Ⓣ Ⓦ Ⓣ Ⓕ Ⓢ

MOOD:
- ☐ Chatty
- ☐ Happy
- ☐ Cranky
- ☐ Playful
- ☐ Cuddly
- ☐ Quiet
- ☐ Friendly
- ☐ Sad
- ☐ Fussy
- ☐ Sick
- ☐ Grumpy
- ☐ Sleepy
- ☐ Other: _____

NOTES FROM PARENT(S):
_____
_____
_____
_____

WOKE UP AT:
A.M.
P.M.

LAST FED AT:
A.M.
P.M.

MEALS:

	TIME
Breakfast	
Snack	
Lunch	
Snack	
Dinner	

POTTY:

Time	Diaper	Potty	Dry	Wet	BM
___	☐	☐	☐	☐	☐
___	☐	☐	☐	☐	☐
___	☐	☐	☐	☐	☐
___	☐	☐	☐	☐	☐
___	☐	☐	☐	☐	☐
___	☐	☐	☐	☐	☐
___	☐	☐	☐	☐	☐

ACTIVITIES:
- ☐ FREE PLAY
- ☐ READING
- ☐ ARTS/CRAFTS
- ☐ MUSIC/SINGING
- ☐ OUTDOORS PLAY
- ☐ TV/MOVIE
- ☐ FIELD TRIP
- ☐ PLAYDATE WITH _____
- ☐ OTHER _____

SLEEP:

FROM	TO

ACCIDENT REPORT:

ACCIDENT	CARE GIVEN

MEDICATION(S):

TIME	TYPE	AMOUNT

SUPPLIES NEEDED:
_____
_____
_____
_____
_____

NOTES TO PARENTS:
_____
_____
_____
_____
_____

TIME IN: _____   TIME OUT: _____

TODDLER REPORT

CHILD'S NAME: _____

DATE: _____

Ⓢ Ⓜ Ⓣ Ⓦ Ⓣ Ⓕ Ⓢ

MOOD:
- ☐ Chatty
- ☐ Happy
- ☐ Cranky
- ☐ Playful
- ☐ Cuddly
- ☐ Quiet
- ☐ Friendly
- ☐ Sad
- ☐ Fussy
- ☐ Sick
- ☐ Grumpy
- ☐ Sleepy
- ☐ Other: _____

NOTES FROM PARENT(S):
_____
_____
_____
_____

WOKE UP AT:
A.M.
P.M.

LAST FED AT:
A.M.
P.M.

MEALS:

	TIME
Breakfast	
Snack	
Lunch	
Snack	
Dinner	

POTTY:

Time	Diaper	Potty	Dry	Wet	BM
___	☐	☐	☐	☐	☐
___	☐	☐	☐	☐	☐
___	☐	☐	☐	☐	☐
___	☐	☐	☐	☐	☐
___	☐	☐	☐	☐	☐
___	☐	☐	☐	☐	☐
___	☐	☐	☐	☐	☐

ACTIVITIES:
- ☐ FREE PLAY
- ☐ READING
- ☐ ARTS/CRAFTS
- ☐ MUSIC/SINGING
- ☐ OUTDOORS PLAY
- ☐ TV/MOVIE
- ☐ FIELD TRIP
- ☐ PLAYDATE WITH _____
- ☐ OTHER _____

SLEEP:

FROM	TO

ACCIDENT REPORT:

ACCIDENT	CARE GIVEN

MEDICATION(S):

TIME	TYPE	AMOUNT

SUPPLIES NEEDED:
_____
_____
_____
_____

NOTES TO PARENTS:
_____
_____
_____
_____

TIME IN: _____ TIME OUT: _____

TODDLER REPORT

CHILD'S NAME:

DATE:

Ⓢ Ⓜ Ⓣ Ⓦ Ⓣ Ⓕ Ⓢ

MOOD:
- ☐ Chatty
- ☐ Happy
- ☐ Cranky
- ☐ Playful
- ☐ Cuddly
- ☐ Quiet
- ☐ Friendly
- ☐ Sad
- ☐ Fussy
- ☐ Sick
- ☐ Grumpy
- ☐ Sleepy
- ☐ Other: _____

NOTES FROM PARENT(S):
_____
_____
_____
_____

WOKE UP AT:
A.M.
P.M.

LAST FED AT:
A.M.
P.M.

MEALS:

	TIME
Breakfast	
Snack	
Lunch	
Snack	
Dinner	

POTTY:

Time	Diaper	Potty	Dry	Wet	BM
____	☐	☐	☐	☐	☐
____	☐	☐	☐	☐	☐
____	☐	☐	☐	☐	☐
____	☐	☐	☐	☐	☐
____	☐	☐	☐	☐	☐
____	☐	☐	☐	☐	☐
____	☐	☐	☐	☐	☐

ACTIVITIES:
- ☐ FREE PLAY
- ☐ READING
- ☐ ARTS/CRAFTS
- ☐ MUSIC/SINGING
- ☐ OUTDOORS PLAY
- ☐ TV/MOVIE
- ☐ FIELD TRIP
- ☐ PLAYDATE WITH _____
- ☐ OTHER _____

SLEEP:

FROM	TO

ACCIDENT REPORT:

ACCIDENT	CARE GIVEN

MEDICATION(S):

TIME	TYPE	AMOUNT

SUPPLIES NEEDED:
_____
_____
_____
_____
_____

NOTES TO PARENTS:
_____
_____
_____
_____
_____

TIME IN: **TIME OUT:**

TODDLER REPORT

DATE:

CHILD'S NAME:

Ⓢ Ⓜ Ⓣ Ⓦ Ⓣ Ⓕ Ⓢ

MOOD:
- ☐ Chatty
- ☐ Happy
- ☐ Cranky
- ☐ Playful
- ☐ Cuddly
- ☐ Quiet
- ☐ Friendly
- ☐ Sad
- ☐ Fussy
- ☐ Sick
- ☐ Grumpy
- ☐ Sleepy
- ☐ Other: _____

NOTES FROM PARENT(S):

WOKE UP AT:
A.M.
P.M.

LAST FED AT:
A.M.
P.M.

MEALS:

	TIME
Breakfast	
Snack	
Lunch	
Snack	
Dinner	

POTTY:

Time	Diaper	Potty	Dry	Wet	BM
___	☐	☐	☐	☐	☐
___	☐	☐	☐	☐	☐
___	☐	☐	☐	☐	☐
___	☐	☐	☐	☐	☐
___	☐	☐	☐	☐	☐
___	☐	☐	☐	☐	☐
___	☐	☐	☐	☐	☐

ACTIVITIES:
- ☐ FREE PLAY
- ☐ READING
- ☐ ARTS/CRAFTS
- ☐ MUSIC/SINGING
- ☐ OUTDOORS PLAY
- ☐ TV/MOVIE
- ☐ FIELD TRIP
- ☐ PLAYDATE WITH _____
- ☐ OTHER _____

SLEEP:

FROM	TO

ACCIDENT REPORT:

ACCIDENT	CARE GIVEN

MEDICATION(S):

TIME	TYPE	AMOUNT

SUPPLIES NEEDED:

NOTES TO PARENTS:

TIME IN: TIME OUT:

TODDLER REPORT

CHILD'S NAME: _____

DATE: _____

Ⓢ Ⓜ Ⓣ Ⓦ Ⓣ Ⓕ Ⓢ

MOOD:
- ☐ Chatty
- ☐ Happy
- ☐ Cranky
- ☐ Playful
- ☐ Cuddly
- ☐ Quiet
- ☐ Friendly
- ☐ Sad
- ☐ Fussy
- ☐ Sick
- ☐ Grumpy
- ☐ Sleepy
- ☐ Other: _____

NOTES FROM PARENT(S):
_____
_____
_____
_____

WOKE UP AT:
_____ A.M. / P.M.

LAST FED AT:
_____ A.M. / P.M.

MEALS:

	TIME
Breakfast	
Snack	
Lunch	
Snack	
Dinner	

POTTY:

Time	Diaper	Potty	Dry	Wet	BM
	☐	☐	☐	☐	☐
	☐	☐	☐	☐	☐
	☐	☐	☐	☐	☐
	☐	☐	☐	☐	☐
	☐	☐	☐	☐	☐
	☐	☐	☐	☐	☐
	☐	☐	☐	☐	☐

ACTIVITIES:
- ☐ FREE PLAY
- ☐ READING
- ☐ ARTS/CRAFTS
- ☐ MUSIC/SINGING
- ☐ OUTDOORS PLAY
- ☐ TV/MOVIE
- ☐ FIELD TRIP
- ☐ PLAYDATE WITH _____
- ☐ OTHER _____

SLEEP:

FROM	TO

ACCIDENT REPORT:

ACCIDENT	CARE GIVEN

MEDICATION(S):

TIME	TYPE	AMOUNT

SUPPLIES NEEDED:
_____
_____
_____
_____
_____

NOTES TO PARENTS:
_____
_____
_____
_____
_____
_____

TIME IN: _____   **TIME OUT:** _____

TODDLER REPORT

DATE: _____

CHILD'S NAME: _____

(S) (M) (T) (W) (T) (F) (S)

MOOD:
- ☐ Chatty
- ☐ Happy
- ☐ Cranky
- ☐ Playful
- ☐ Cuddly
- ☐ Quiet
- ☐ Friendly
- ☐ Sad
- ☐ Fussy
- ☐ Sick
- ☐ Grumpy
- ☐ Sleepy
- ☐ Other: _____

NOTES FROM PARENT(S):
_____
_____
_____
_____
_____

WOKE UP AT:
A.M.
P.M.

LAST FED AT:
A.M.
P.M.

MEALS:

	TIME
Breakfast	
Snack	
Lunch	
Snack	
Dinner	

POTTY:

Time	Diaper	Potty	Dry	Wet	BM
	☐	☐	☐	☐	☐
	☐	☐	☐	☐	☐
	☐	☐	☐	☐	☐
	☐	☐	☐	☐	☐
	☐	☐	☐	☐	☐
	☐	☐	☐	☐	☐
	☐	☐	☐	☐	☐

ACTIVITIES:
- ☐ FREE PLAY
- ☐ READING
- ☐ ARTS/CRAFTS
- ☐ MUSIC/SINGING
- ☐ OUTDOORS PLAY
- ☐ TV/MOVIE
- ☐ FIELD TRIP
- ☐ PLAYDATE WITH _____
- ☐ OTHER _____

SLEEP:

FROM	TO

ACCIDENT REPORT:

ACCIDENT	CARE GIVEN

MEDICATION(S):

TIME	TYPE	AMOUNT

SUPPLIES NEEDED:
_____
_____
_____
_____
_____

NOTES TO PARENTS:
_____
_____
_____
_____
_____

TIME IN: _____ TIME OUT: _____

TODDLER REPORT

CHILD'S NAME:

DATE:

Ⓢ Ⓜ Ⓣ Ⓦ Ⓣ Ⓕ Ⓢ

MOOD:
- ☐ Chatty
- ☐ Happy
- ☐ Cranky
- ☐ Playful
- ☐ Cuddly
- ☐ Quiet
- ☐ Friendly
- ☐ Sad
- ☐ Fussy
- ☐ Sick
- ☐ Grumpy
- ☐ Sleepy
- ☐ Other: _____

NOTES FROM PARENT(S):
_____
_____
_____
_____

WOKE UP AT:
A.M.
P.M.

LAST FED AT:
A.M.
P.M.

MEALS:

	TIME
Breakfast	
Snack	
Lunch	
Snack	
Dinner	

POTTY:

Time	Diaper	Potty	Dry	Wet	BM
___	☐	☐	☐	☐	☐
___	☐	☐	☐	☐	☐
___	☐	☐	☐	☐	☐
___	☐	☐	☐	☐	☐
___	☐	☐	☐	☐	☐
___	☐	☐	☐	☐	☐
___	☐	☐	☐	☐	☐

ACTIVITIES:
- ☐ FREE PLAY
- ☐ READING
- ☐ ARTS/CRAFTS
- ☐ MUSIC/SINGING
- ☐ OUTDOORS PLAY
- ☐ TV/MOVIE
- ☐ FIELD TRIP
- ☐ PLAYDATE WITH _____
- ☐ OTHER _____

SLEEP:

FROM	TO

ACCIDENT REPORT:

ACCIDENT	CARE GIVEN

MEDICATION(S):

TIME	TYPE	AMOUNT

SUPPLIES NEEDED:
_____
_____
_____
_____
_____

NOTES TO PARENTS:
_____
_____
_____
_____
_____

TIME IN: **TIME OUT:**

TODDLER REPORT

CHILD'S NAME:

DATE:

Ⓢ Ⓜ Ⓣ Ⓦ Ⓣ Ⓕ Ⓢ

MOOD:
- ☐ Chatty
- ☐ Happy
- ☐ Cranky
- ☐ Playful
- ☐ Cuddly
- ☐ Quiet
- ☐ Friendly
- ☐ Sad
- ☐ Fussy
- ☐ Sick
- ☐ Grumpy
- ☐ Sleepy
- ☐ Other: _____

NOTES FROM PARENT(S):
_____
_____
_____
_____

WOKE UP AT:
A.M.
P.M.

LAST FED AT:
A.M.
P.M.

MEALS:

	TIME
Breakfast	
Snack	
Lunch	
Snack	
Dinner	

POTTY:

Time	Diaper	Potty	Dry	Wet	BM
___	☐	☐	☐	☐	☐
___	☐	☐	☐	☐	☐
___	☐	☐	☐	☐	☐
___	☐	☐	☐	☐	☐
___	☐	☐	☐	☐	☐
___	☐	☐	☐	☐	☐
___	☐	☐	☐	☐	☐

ACTIVITIES:
- ☐ FREE PLAY
- ☐ READING
- ☐ ARTS/CRAFTS
- ☐ MUSIC/SINGING
- ☐ OUTDOORS PLAY
- ☐ TV/MOVIE
- ☐ FIELD TRIP
- ☐ PLAYDATE WITH _____
- ☐ OTHER _____

SLEEP:

FROM	TO

ACCIDENT REPORT:

ACCIDENT	CARE GIVEN

MEDICATION(S):

TIME	TYPE	AMOUNT

SUPPLIES NEEDED:
_____
_____
_____
_____
_____
_____

NOTES TO PARENTS:
_____
_____
_____
_____
_____

TIME IN: _____   TIME OUT: _____

TODDLER REPORT

CHILD'S NAME:

DATE:

(S) (M) (T) (W) (T) (F) (S)

MOOD:
- [ ] Chatty
- [ ] Happy
- [ ] Cranky
- [ ] Playful
- [ ] Cuddly
- [ ] Quiet
- [ ] Friendly
- [ ] Sad
- [ ] Fussy
- [ ] Sick
- [ ] Grumpy
- [ ] Sleepy
- [ ] Other: _____

NOTES FROM PARENT(S):

WOKE UP AT:
A.M.
P.M.

LAST FED AT:
A.M.
P.M.

MEALS:

	TIME
Breakfast	
Snack	
Lunch	
Snack	
Dinner	

POTTY:

Time	Diaper	Potty	Dry	Wet	BM
___	☐	☐	☐	☐	☐
___	☐	☐	☐	☐	☐
___	☐	☐	☐	☐	☐
___	☐	☐	☐	☐	☐
___	☐	☐	☐	☐	☐
___	☐	☐	☐	☐	☐
___	☐	☐	☐	☐	☐

ACTIVITIES:
- [ ] FREE PLAY
- [ ] READING
- [ ] ARTS/CRAFTS
- [ ] MUSIC/SINGING
- [ ] OUTDOORS PLAY
- [ ] TV/MOVIE
- [ ] FIELD TRIP
- [ ] PLAYDATE WITH _____
- [ ] OTHER _____

SLEEP:

FROM	TO

ACCIDENT REPORT:

ACCIDENT	CARE GIVEN

MEDICATION(S):

TIME	TYPE	AMOUNT

SUPPLIES NEEDED:

NOTES TO PARENTS:

TIME IN: **TIME OUT:**

TODDLER REPORT

CHILD'S NAME:

DATE:

Ⓢ Ⓜ Ⓣ Ⓦ Ⓣ Ⓕ Ⓢ

MOOD:
- ☐ Chatty
- ☐ Happy
- ☐ Cranky
- ☐ Playful
- ☐ Cuddly
- ☐ Quiet
- ☐ Friendly
- ☐ Sad
- ☐ Fussy
- ☐ Sick
- ☐ Grumpy
- ☐ Sleepy
- ☐ Other: _____

NOTES FROM PARENT(S):
_____
_____
_____
_____

WOKE UP AT:
A.M.
P.M.

LAST FED AT:
A.M.
P.M.

MEALS:
	TIME
Breakfast	
Snack	
Lunch	
Snack	
Dinner	

POTTY:
Time	Diaper	Potty	Dry	Wet	BM
	☐	☐	☐	☐	☐
	☐	☐	☐	☐	☐
	☐	☐	☐	☐	☐
	☐	☐	☐	☐	☐
	☐	☐	☐	☐	☐
	☐	☐	☐	☐	☐
	☐	☐	☐	☐	☐

ACTIVITIES:
- ☐ FREE PLAY
- ☐ READING
- ☐ ARTS/CRAFTS
- ☐ MUSIC/SINGING
- ☐ OUTDOORS PLAY
- ☐ TV/MOVIE
- ☐ FIELD TRIP
- ☐ PLAYDATE WITH _____
- ☐ OTHER _____

SLEEP:
FROM	TO

ACCIDENT REPORT:
ACCIDENT	CARE GIVEN

MEDICATION(S):
TIME	TYPE	AMOUNT

SUPPLIES NEEDED:
_____
_____
_____
_____
_____
_____

NOTES TO PARENTS:
_____
_____
_____
_____
_____

TIME IN: **TIME OUT:**

TODDLER REPORT

CHILD'S NAME:

DATE:

S M T W T F S

MOOD:
- ☐ Chatty
- ☐ Happy
- ☐ Cranky
- ☐ Playful
- ☐ Cuddly
- ☐ Quiet
- ☐ Friendly
- ☐ Sad
- ☐ Fussy
- ☐ Sick
- ☐ Grumpy
- ☐ Sleepy
- ☐ Other: _____

NOTES FROM PARENT(S):

WOKE UP AT:
A.M.
P.M.

LAST FED AT:
A.M.
P.M.

MEALS:
	TIME
Breakfast	
Snack	
Lunch	
Snack	
Dinner	

POTTY:
Time	Diaper	Potty	Dry	Wet	BM
	☐	☐	☐	☐	☐
	☐	☐	☐	☐	☐
	☐	☐	☐	☐	☐
	☐	☐	☐	☐	☐
	☐	☐	☐	☐	☐
	☐	☐	☐	☐	☐
	☐	☐	☐	☐	☐

ACTIVITIES:
- ☐ FREE PLAY
- ☐ READING
- ☐ ARTS/CRAFTS
- ☐ MUSIC/SINGING
- ☐ OUTDOORS PLAY
- ☐ TV/MOVIE
- ☐ FIELD TRIP
- ☐ PLAYDATE WITH _____
- ☐ OTHER _____

SLEEP:
FROM	TO

ACCIDENT REPORT:
ACCIDENT	CARE GIVEN

MEDICATION(S):
TIME	TYPE	AMOUNT

SUPPLIES NEEDED:

NOTES TO PARENTS:

TIME IN: TIME OUT:

TODDLER REPORT

DATE:

CHILD'S NAME:

(S) (M) (T) (W) (T) (F) (S)

MOOD:
- ☐ Chatty
- ☐ Happy
- ☐ Cranky
- ☐ Playful
- ☐ Cuddly
- ☐ Quiet
- ☐ Friendly
- ☐ Sad
- ☐ Fussy
- ☐ Sick
- ☐ Grumpy
- ☐ Sleepy
- ☐ Other: _____

NOTES FROM PARENT(S):

WOKE UP AT:
A.M.
P.M.

LAST FED AT:
A.M.
P.M.

MEALS:

	TIME
Breakfast	
Snack	
Lunch	
Snack	
Dinner	

POTTY:

Time	Diaper	Potty	Dry	Wet	BM
	☐	☐	☐	☐	☐
	☐	☐	☐	☐	☐
	☐	☐	☐	☐	☐
	☐	☐	☐	☐	☐
	☐	☐	☐	☐	☐
	☐	☐	☐	☐	☐
	☐	☐	☐	☐	☐

ACTIVITIES:
- ☐ FREE PLAY
- ☐ READING
- ☐ ARTS/CRAFTS
- ☐ MUSIC/SINGING
- ☐ OUTDOORS PLAY
- ☐ TV/MOVIE
- ☐ FIELD TRIP
- ☐ PLAYDATE WITH _____
- ☐ OTHER _____

SLEEP:

FROM	TO

ACCIDENT REPORT:

ACCIDENT	CARE GIVEN

MEDICATION(S):

TIME	TYPE	AMOUNT

SUPPLIES NEEDED:

NOTES TO PARENTS:

TIME IN: **TIME OUT:**

TODDLER REPORT

CHILD'S NAME:

DATE:

Ⓢ Ⓜ Ⓣ Ⓦ Ⓣ Ⓕ Ⓢ

MOOD:
- ☐ Chatty
- ☐ Happy
- ☐ Cranky
- ☐ Playful
- ☐ Cuddly
- ☐ Quiet
- ☐ Friendly
- ☐ Sad
- ☐ Fussy
- ☐ Sick
- ☐ Grumpy
- ☐ Sleepy
- ☐ Other: _____

NOTES FROM PARENT(S):

WOKE UP AT:
A.M.
P.M.

LAST FED AT:
A.M.
P.M.

MEALS:

	TIME
Breakfast	
Snack	
Lunch	
Snack	
Dinner	

POTTY:

Time	Diaper	Potty	Dry	Wet	BM
___	☐	☐	☐	☐	☐
___	☐	☐	☐	☐	☐
___	☐	☐	☐	☐	☐
___	☐	☐	☐	☐	☐
___	☐	☐	☐	☐	☐
___	☐	☐	☐	☐	☐
___	☐	☐	☐	☐	☐

ACTIVITIES:
- ☐ FREE PLAY
- ☐ READING
- ☐ ARTS/CRAFTS
- ☐ MUSIC/SINGING
- ☐ OUTDOORS PLAY
- ☐ TV/MOVIE
- ☐ FIELD TRIP
- ☐ PLAYDATE WITH _____
- ☐ OTHER _____

SLEEP:

FROM	TO

ACCIDENT REPORT:

ACCIDENT	CARE GIVEN

MEDICATION(S):

TIME	TYPE	AMOUNT

SUPPLIES NEEDED:

NOTES TO PARENTS:

TIME IN: **TIME OUT:**

TODDLER REPORT

DATE:

CHILD'S NAME:

(S) (M) (T) (W) (T) (F) (S)

MOOD:
- ☐ Chatty
- ☐ Happy
- ☐ Cranky
- ☐ Playful
- ☐ Cuddly
- ☐ Quiet
- ☐ Friendly
- ☐ Sad
- ☐ Fussy
- ☐ Sick
- ☐ Grumpy
- ☐ Sleepy
- ☐ Other: _____

NOTES FROM PARENT(S):

WOKE UP AT:
A.M.
P.M.

LAST FED AT:
A.M.
P.M.

MEALS:

	TIME
Breakfast	
Snack	
Lunch	
Snack	
Dinner	

POTTY:

Time	Diaper	Potty	Dry	Wet	BM
___	☐	☐	☐	☐	☐
___	☐	☐	☐	☐	☐
___	☐	☐	☐	☐	☐
___	☐	☐	☐	☐	☐
___	☐	☐	☐	☐	☐
___	☐	☐	☐	☐	☐
___	☐	☐	☐	☐	☐

ACTIVITIES:
- ☐ FREE PLAY
- ☐ READING
- ☐ ARTS/CRAFTS
- ☐ MUSIC/SINGING
- ☐ OUTDOORS PLAY
- ☐ TV/MOVIE
- ☐ FIELD TRIP
- ☐ PLAYDATE WITH _____
- ☐ OTHER _____

SLEEP:

FROM	TO

ACCIDENT REPORT:

ACCIDENT	CARE GIVEN

MEDICATION(S):

TIME	TYPE	AMOUNT

SUPPLIES NEEDED:

NOTES TO PARENTS:

TIME IN: **TIME OUT:**

TODDLER REPORT

CHILD'S NAME:

DATE:

S M T W T F S

MOOD:
- ☐ Chatty
- ☐ Happy
- ☐ Cranky
- ☐ Playful
- ☐ Cuddly
- ☐ Quiet
- ☐ Friendly
- ☐ Sad
- ☐ Fussy
- ☐ Sick
- ☐ Grumpy
- ☐ Sleepy
- ☐ Other: _____

NOTES FROM PARENT(S):

WOKE UP AT:
A.M.
P.M.

LAST FED AT:
A.M.
P.M.

MEALS:

	TIME
Breakfast	
Snack	
Lunch	
Snack	
Dinner	

POTTY:

Time	Diaper	Potty	Dry	Wet	BM
	☐	☐	☐	☐	☐
	☐	☐	☐	☐	☐
	☐	☐	☐	☐	☐
	☐	☐	☐	☐	☐
	☐	☐	☐	☐	☐
	☐	☐	☐	☐	☐
	☐	☐	☐	☐	☐

ACTIVITIES:
- ☐ FREE PLAY
- ☐ READING
- ☐ ARTS/CRAFTS
- ☐ MUSIC/SINGING
- ☐ OUTDOORS PLAY
- ☐ TV/MOVIE
- ☐ FIELD TRIP
- ☐ PLAYDATE WITH _____
- ☐ OTHER _____

SLEEP:

FROM	TO

ACCIDENT REPORT:

ACCIDENT	CARE GIVEN

MEDICATION(S):

TIME	TYPE	AMOUNT

SUPPLIES NEEDED:

NOTES TO PARENTS:

TIME IN: **TIME OUT:**

TODDLER REPORT

CHILD'S NAME:

DATE:

Ⓢ Ⓜ Ⓣ Ⓦ Ⓣ Ⓕ Ⓢ

MOOD:
- ☐ Chatty
- ☐ Happy
- ☐ Cranky
- ☐ Playful
- ☐ Cuddly
- ☐ Quiet
- ☐ Friendly
- ☐ Sad
- ☐ Fussy
- ☐ Sick
- ☐ Grumpy
- ☐ Sleepy
- ☐ Other: _____

NOTES FROM PARENT(S):

WOKE UP AT:
A.M.
P.M.

LAST FED AT:
A.M.
P.M.

MEALS:

	TIME
Breakfast	
Snack	
Lunch	
Snack	
Dinner	

POTTY:

Time	Diaper	Potty	Dry	Wet	BM
	☐	☐	☐	☐	☐
	☐	☐	☐	☐	☐
	☐	☐	☐	☐	☐
	☐	☐	☐	☐	☐
	☐	☐	☐	☐	☐
	☐	☐	☐	☐	☐
	☐	☐	☐	☐	☐

ACTIVITIES:
- ☐ FREE PLAY
- ☐ READING
- ☐ ARTS/CRAFTS
- ☐ MUSIC/SINGING
- ☐ OUTDOORS PLAY
- ☐ TV/MOVIE
- ☐ FIELD TRIP
- ☐ PLAYDATE WITH _____
- ☐ OTHER _____

SLEEP:

FROM	TO

ACCIDENT REPORT:

ACCIDENT	CARE GIVEN

MEDICATION(S):

TIME	TYPE	AMOUNT

SUPPLIES NEEDED:

NOTES TO PARENTS:

TIME IN:

TIME OUT:

TODDLER REPORT

CHILD'S NAME:

DATE:

(S) (M) (T) (W) (T) (F) (S)

MOOD:
- ☐ Chatty
- ☐ Happy
- ☐ Cranky
- ☐ Playful
- ☐ Cuddly
- ☐ Quiet
- ☐ Friendly
- ☐ Sad
- ☐ Fussy
- ☐ Sick
- ☐ Grumpy
- ☐ Sleepy
- ☐ Other: _____

NOTES FROM PARENT(S):
_____
_____
_____
_____

WOKE UP AT:
A.M.
P.M.

LAST FED AT:
A.M.
P.M.

MEALS:

	TIME
Breakfast	
Snack	
Lunch	
Snack	
Dinner	

POTTY:

Time	Diaper	Potty	Dry	Wet	BM
___	☐	☐	☐	☐	☐
___	☐	☐	☐	☐	☐
___	☐	☐	☐	☐	☐
___	☐	☐	☐	☐	☐
___	☐	☐	☐	☐	☐
___	☐	☐	☐	☐	☐
___	☐	☐	☐	☐	☐

ACTIVITIES:
- ☐ FREE PLAY
- ☐ READING
- ☐ ARTS/CRAFTS
- ☐ MUSIC/SINGING
- ☐ OUTDOORS PLAY
- ☐ TV/MOVIE
- ☐ FIELD TRIP
- ☐ PLAYDATE WITH _____
- ☐ OTHER _____

SLEEP:

FROM	TO

ACCIDENT REPORT:

ACCIDENT	CARE GIVEN

MEDICATION(S):

TIME	TYPE	AMOUNT

SUPPLIES NEEDED:
_____
_____
_____
_____
_____

NOTES TO PARENTS:
_____
_____
_____
_____
_____

TIME IN: TIME OUT:

TODDLER REPORT

CHILD'S NAME:

DATE:

Ⓢ Ⓜ Ⓣ Ⓦ Ⓣ Ⓕ Ⓢ

MOOD:
- ☐ Chatty
- ☐ Cranky
- ☐ Cuddly
- ☐ Friendly
- ☐ Fussy
- ☐ Grumpy
- ☐ Happy
- ☐ Playful
- ☐ Quiet
- ☐ Sad
- ☐ Sick
- ☐ Sleepy
- ☐ Other: _____

NOTES FROM PARENT(S).

WOKE UP AT:
A.M.
P.M.

LAST FED AT:
A.M.
P.M.

MEALS:
	TIME
Breakfast	
Snack	
Lunch	
Snack	
Dinner	

POTTY:
Time	Diaper	Potty	Dry	Wet	BM
	☐	☐	☐	☐	☐
	☐	☐	☐	☐	☐
	☐	☐	☐	☐	☐
	☐	☐	☐	☐	☐
	☐	☐	☐	☐	☐
	☐	☐	☐	☐	☐
	☐	☐	☐	☐	☐

ACTIVITIES:
- ☐ FREE PLAY
- ☐ READING
- ☐ ARTS/CRAFTS
- ☐ MUSIC/SINGING
- ☐ OUTDOORS PLAY
- ☐ TV/MOVIE
- ☐ FIELD TRIP
- ☐ PLAYDATE WITH _____
- ☐ OTHER _____

SLEEP:
FROM	TO

ACCIDENT REPORT:
ACCIDENT	CARE GIVEN

MEDICATION(S):
TIME	TYPE	AMOUNT

SUPPLIES NEEDED:

NOTES TO PARENTS:

TIME IN: TIME OUT:

TODDLER REPORT

CHILD'S NAME: _____

DATE: _____

Ⓢ Ⓜ Ⓣ Ⓦ Ⓣ Ⓕ Ⓢ

MOOD:
- ☐ Chatty
- ☐ Happy
- ☐ Cranky
- ☐ Playful
- ☐ Cuddly
- ☐ Quiet
- ☐ Friendly
- ☐ Sad
- ☐ Fussy
- ☐ Sick
- ☐ Grumpy
- ☐ Sleepy
- ☐ Other: _____

NOTES FROM PARENT(S):
_____
_____
_____
_____

WOKE UP AT:
_____ A.M. / P.M.

LAST FED AT:
_____ A.M. / P.M.

MEALS:

	TIME
Breakfast	
Snack	
Lunch	
Snack	
Dinner	

POTTY:

Time	Diaper	Potty	Dry	Wet	BM
___	☐	☐	☐	☐	☐
___	☐	☐	☐	☐	☐
___	☐	☐	☐	☐	☐
___	☐	☐	☐	☐	☐
___	☐	☐	☐	☐	☐
___	☐	☐	☐	☐	☐
___	☐	☐	☐	☐	☐

ACTIVITIES:
- ☐ FREE PLAY
- ☐ READING
- ☐ ARTS/CRAFTS
- ☐ MUSIC/SINGING
- ☐ OUTDOORS PLAY
- ☐ TV/MOVIE
- ☐ FIELD TRIP
- ☐ PLAYDATE WITH _____
- ☐ OTHER _____

SLEEP:

FROM	TO

ACCIDENT REPORT:

ACCIDENT	CARE GIVEN

MEDICATION(S):

TIME	TYPE	AMOUNT

SUPPLIES NEEDED:
_____
_____
_____
_____
_____

NOTES TO PARENTS:
_____
_____
_____
_____
_____

TIME IN: _____ TIME OUT: _____

TODDLER REPORT

DATE: _____

CHILD'S NAME: _____

Ⓢ Ⓜ Ⓣ Ⓦ Ⓣ Ⓕ Ⓢ

MOOD:
- ☐ Chatty
- ☐ Cranky
- ☐ Cuddly
- ☐ Friendly
- ☐ Fussy
- ☐ Grumpy
- ☐ Happy
- ☐ Playful
- ☐ Quiet
- ☐ Sad
- ☐ Sick
- ☐ Sleepy
- ☐ Other: _____

NOTES FROM PARENT(S):
_____
_____
_____
_____

WOKE UP AT:
_____ A.M. / P.M.

LAST FED AT:
_____ A.M. / P.M.

MEALS:

	TIME
Breakfast	
Snack	
Lunch	
Snack	
Dinner	

POTTY:

Time	Diaper	Potty	Dry	Wet	BM
____	☐	☐	☐	☐	☐
____	☐	☐	☐	☐	☐
____	☐	☐	☐	☐	☐
____	☐	☐	☐	☐	☐
____	☐	☐	☐	☐	☐
____	☐	☐	☐	☐	☐
____	☐	☐	☐	☐	☐

ACTIVITIES:
- ☐ FREE PLAY
- ☐ READING
- ☐ ARTS/CRAFTS
- ☐ MUSIC/SINGING
- ☐ OUTDOORS PLAY
- ☐ TV/MOVIE
- ☐ FIELD TRIP
- ☐ PLAYDATE WITH _____
- ☐ OTHER _____

SLEEP:

FROM	TO

ACCIDENT REPORT:

ACCIDENT	CARE GIVEN

MEDICATION(S):

TIME	TYPE	AMOUNT

SUPPLIES NEEDED:
_____
_____
_____
_____
_____

NOTES TO PARENTS:
_____
_____
_____
_____
_____

TIME IN: _____   TIME OUT: _____

TODDLER REPORT

DATE: _____

CHILD'S NAME: _____

Ⓢ Ⓜ Ⓣ Ⓦ Ⓣ Ⓕ Ⓢ

MOOD:
- ☐ Chatty
- ☐ Happy
- ☐ Cranky
- ☐ Playful
- ☐ Cuddly
- ☐ Quiet
- ☐ Friendly
- ☐ Sad
- ☐ Fussy
- ☐ Sick
- ☐ Grumpy
- ☐ Sleepy
- ☐ Other: _____

NOTES FROM PARENT(S):
_____
_____
_____
_____
_____

WOKE UP AT:
_____ A.M. P.M.

LAST FED AT:
_____ A.M. P.M.

MEALS:

	TIME
Breakfast	
Snack	
Lunch	
Snack	
Dinner	

POTTY:

Time	Diaper	Potty	Dry	Wet	BM
_____	☐	☐	☐	☐	☐
_____	☐	☐	☐	☐	☐
_____	☐	☐	☐	☐	☐
_____	☐	☐	☐	☐	☐
_____	☐	☐	☐	☐	☐
_____	☐	☐	☐	☐	☐
_____	☐	☐	☐	☐	☐

ACTIVITIES:
- ☐ FREE PLAY
- ☐ READING
- ☐ ARTS/CRAFTS
- ☐ MUSIC/SINGING
- ☐ OUTDOORS PLAY
- ☐ TV/MOVIE
- ☐ FIELD TRIP
- ☐ PLAYDATE WITH _____
- ☐ OTHER _____

SLEEP:

FROM	TO

ACCIDENT REPORT:

ACCIDENT	CARE GIVEN

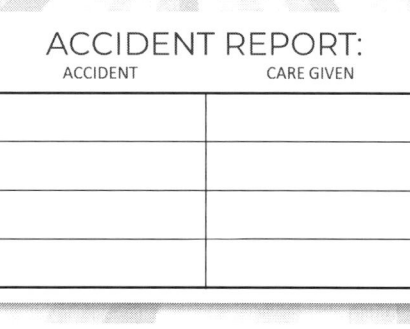

MEDICATION(S):

TIME	TYPE	AMOUNT

SUPPLIES NEEDED:
_____
_____
_____
_____
_____

NOTES TO PARENTS:
_____
_____
_____
_____
_____

TIME IN: _____   TIME OUT: _____

TODDLER REPORT

CHILD'S NAME:

DATE:

Ⓢ Ⓜ Ⓣ Ⓦ Ⓣ Ⓕ Ⓢ

MOOD:
- ☐ Chatty
- ☐ Cranky
- ☐ Cuddly
- ☐ Friendly
- ☐ Fussy
- ☐ Grumpy
- ☐ Happy
- ☐ Playful
- ☐ Quiet
- ☐ Sad
- ☐ Sick
- ☐ Sleepy
- ☐ Other: _____

NOTES FROM PARENT(S):
_____
_____
_____
_____
_____

WOKE UP AT:
A.M.
P.M.

LAST FED AT:
A.M.
P.M.

MEALS:

	TIME
Breakfast	
Snack	
Lunch	
Snack	
Dinner	

POTTY:

Time	Diaper	Potty	Dry	Wet	BM
___	☐	☐	☐	☐	☐
___	☐	☐	☐	☐	☐
___	☐	☐	☐	☐	☐
___	☐	☐	☐	☐	☐
___	☐	☐	☐	☐	☐
___	☐	☐	☐	☐	☐
___	☐	☐	☐	☐	☐

ACTIVITIES:
- ☐ FREE PLAY
- ☐ READING
- ☐ ARTS/CRAFTS
- ☐ MUSIC/SINGING
- ☐ OUTDOORS PLAY
- ☐ TV/MOVIE
- ☐ FIELD TRIP
- ☐ PLAYDATE WITH _____
- ☐ OTHER _____

SLEEP:

FROM	TO

ACCIDENT REPORT:

ACCIDENT	CARE GIVEN

MEDICATION(S):

TIME	TYPE	AMOUNT

SUPPLIES NEEDED:
_____
_____
_____
_____
_____

NOTES TO PARENTS:
_____
_____
_____
_____
_____
_____

TIME IN: **TIME OUT:**

TODDLER REPORT

CHILD'S NAME:

DATE:

Ⓢ Ⓜ Ⓣ Ⓦ Ⓣ Ⓕ Ⓢ

MOOD:
- ☐ Chatty
- ☐ Happy
- ☐ Cranky
- ☐ Playful
- ☐ Cuddly
- ☐ Quiet
- ☐ Friendly
- ☐ Sad
- ☐ Fussy
- ☐ Sick
- ☐ Grumpy
- ☐ Sleepy
- ☐ Other: _____

NOTES FROM PARENT(S):
_____
_____
_____
_____
_____

WOKE UP AT:
A.M.
P.M.

LAST FED AT:
A.M.
P.M.

MEALS:

	TIME
Breakfast	
Snack	
Lunch	
Snack	
Dinner	

POTTY:

Time	Diaper	Potty	Dry	Wet	BM
	☐	☐	☐	☐	☐
	☐	☐	☐	☐	☐
	☐	☐	☐	☐	☐
	☐	☐	☐	☐	☐
	☐	☐	☐	☐	☐
	☐	☐	☐	☐	☐
	☐	☐	☐	☐	☐

ACTIVITIES:
- ☐ FREE PLAY
- ☐ READING
- ☐ ARTS/CRAFTS
- ☐ MUSIC/SINGING
- ☐ OUTDOORS PLAY
- ☐ TV/MOVIE
- ☐ FIELD TRIP
- ☐ PLAYDATE WITH _____
- ☐ OTHER _____

SLEEP:

FROM	TO

ACCIDENT REPORT:

ACCIDENT	CARE GIVEN

MEDICATION(S):

TIME	TYPE	AMOUNT

SUPPLIES NEEDED:
_____
_____
_____
_____
_____

NOTES TO PARENTS:
_____
_____
_____
_____
_____

TIME IN: **TIME OUT:**

TODDLER REPORT

CHILD'S NAME:

DATE:

S M T W T F S

MOOD:
- ☐ Chatty
- ☐ Happy
- ☐ Cranky
- ☐ Playful
- ☐ Cuddly
- ☐ Quiet
- ☐ Friendly
- ☐ Sad
- ☐ Fussy
- ☐ Sick
- ☐ Grumpy
- ☐ Sleepy
- ☐ Other: _____

NOTES FROM PARENT(S):

WOKE UP AT:
A.M.
P.M.

LAST FED AT:
A.M.
P.M.

MEALS:

	TIME
Breakfast	
Snack	
Lunch	
Snack	
Dinner	

POTTY:

Time	Diaper	Potty	Dry	Wet	BM
	☐	☐	☐	☐	☐
	☐	☐	☐	☐	☐
	☐	☐	☐	☐	☐
	☐	☐	☐	☐	☐
	☐	☐	☐	☐	☐
	☐	☐	☐	☐	☐
	☐	☐	☐	☐	☐

ACTIVITIES:
- ☐ FREE PLAY
- ☐ READING
- ☐ ARTS/CRAFTS
- ☐ MUSIC/SINGING
- ☐ OUTDOORS PLAY
- ☐ TV/MOVIE
- ☐ FIELD TRIP
- ☐ PLAYDATE WITH _____
- ☐ OTHER _____

SLEEP:

FROM	TO

ACCIDENT REPORT:

ACCIDENT	CARE GIVEN

MEDICATION(S):

TIME	TYPE	AMOUNT

SUPPLIES NEEDED:

NOTES TO PARENTS:

TIME IN: **TIME OUT:**

TODDLER REPORT

DATE:

CHILD'S NAME:

S M T W T F S

MOOD:
- ☐ Chatty
- ☐ Happy
- ☐ Cranky
- ☐ Playful
- ☐ Cuddly
- ☐ Quiet
- ☐ Friendly
- ☐ Sad
- ☐ Fussy
- ☐ Sick
- ☐ Grumpy
- ☐ Sleepy
- ☐ Other: _____

NOTES FROM PARENT(S):

WOKE UP AT:
A.M.
P.M.

LAST FED AT:
A.M.
P.M.

MEALS:

	TIME
Breakfast	
Snack	
Lunch	
Snack	
Dinner	

POTTY:

Time	Diaper	Potty	Dry	Wet	BM
	☐	☐	☐	☐	☐
	☐	☐	☐	☐	☐
	☐	☐	☐	☐	☐
	☐	☐	☐	☐	☐
	☐	☐	☐	☐	☐
	☐	☐	☐	☐	☐
	☐	☐	☐	☐	☐

ACTIVITIES:
- ☐ FREE PLAY
- ☐ READING
- ☐ ARTS/CRAFTS
- ☐ MUSIC/SINGING
- ☐ OUTDOORS PLAY
- ☐ TV/MOVIE
- ☐ FIELD TRIP
- ☐ PLAYDATE WITH _____
- ☐ OTHER _____

SLEEP:

FROM	TO

ACCIDENT REPORT:

ACCIDENT	CARE GIVEN

MEDICATION(S):

TIME	TYPE	AMOUNT

SUPPLIES NEEDED:

NOTES TO PARENTS:

TIME IN: **TIME OUT:**

TODDLER REPORT

CHILD'S NAME:

DATE:

Ⓢ Ⓜ Ⓣ Ⓦ Ⓣ Ⓕ Ⓢ

MOOD:
- ☐ Chatty
- ☐ Happy
- ☐ Cranky
- ☐ Playful
- ☐ Cuddly
- ☐ Quiet
- ☐ Friendly
- ☐ Sad
- ☐ Fussy
- ☐ Sick
- ☐ Grumpy
- ☐ Sleepy
- ☐ Other: _____

NOTES FROM PARENT(S):

WOKE UP AT:
A.M.
P.M.

LAST FED AT:
A.M.
P.M.

MEALS:

	TIME
Breakfast	
Snack	
Lunch	
Snack	
Dinner	

POTTY:

Time	Diaper	Potty	Dry	Wet	BM
____	☐	☐	☐	☐	☐
____	☐	☐	☐	☐	☐
____	☐	☐	☐	☐	☐
____	☐	☐	☐	☐	☐
____	☐	☐	☐	☐	☐
____	☐	☐	☐	☐	☐
____	☐	☐	☐	☐	☐

ACTIVITIES:
- ☐ FREE PLAY
- ☐ READING
- ☐ ARTS/CRAFTS
- ☐ MUSIC/SINGING
- ☐ OUTDOORS PLAY
- ☐ TV/MOVIE
- ☐ FIELD TRIP
- ☐ PLAYDATE WITH _____
- ☐ OTHER _____

SLEEP:

FROM	TO

ACCIDENT REPORT:

ACCIDENT	CARE GIVEN

MEDICATION(S):

TIME	TYPE	AMOUNT

SUPPLIES NEEDED:

NOTES TO PARENTS:

TIME IN: **TIME OUT:**

TODDLER REPORT

CHILD'S NAME: _____

DATE: _____

(S) (M) (T) (W) (T) (F) (S)

MOOD:
- ☐ Chatty
- ☐ Happy
- ☐ Cranky
- ☐ Playful
- ☐ Cuddly
- ☐ Quiet
- ☐ Friendly
- ☐ Sad
- ☐ Fussy
- ☐ Sick
- ☐ Grumpy
- ☐ Sleepy
- ☐ Other: _____

NOTES FROM PARENT(S):
_____
_____
_____
_____
_____

WOKE UP AT:
A.M.
P.M.

LAST FED AT:
A.M.
P.M.

MEALS:

	TIME
Breakfast	
Snack	
Lunch	
Snack	
Dinner	

POTTY:

Time	Diaper	Potty	Dry	Wet	BM
____	☐	☐	☐	☐	☐
____	☐	☐	☐	☐	☐
____	☐	☐	☐	☐	☐
____	☐	☐	☐	☐	☐
____	☐	☐	☐	☐	☐
____	☐	☐	☐	☐	☐
____	☐	☐	☐	☐	☐

ACTIVITIES:
- ☐ FREE PLAY
- ☐ READING
- ☐ ARTS/CRAFTS
- ☐ MUSIC/SINGING
- ☐ OUTDOORS PLAY
- ☐ TV/MOVIE
- ☐ FIELD TRIP
- ☐ PLAYDATE WITH _____
- ☐ OTHER _____

SLEEP:

FROM	TO

ACCIDENT REPORT:

ACCIDENT	CARE GIVEN

MEDICATION(S):

TIME	TYPE	AMOUNT

SUPPLIES NEEDED:
_____
_____
_____
_____
_____
_____

NOTES TO PARENTS:
_____
_____
_____
_____
_____
_____

TIME IN: _____ TIME OUT: _____

TODDLER REPORT

CHILD'S NAME:

DATE:

S M T W T F S

MOOD:
- [ ] Chatty
- [ ] Cranky
- [ ] Cuddly
- [ ] Friendly
- [ ] Fussy
- [ ] Grumpy
- [ ] Happy
- [ ] Playful
- [ ] Quiet
- [ ] Sad
- [ ] Sick
- [ ] Sleepy
- [ ] Other: _____

NOTES FROM PARENT(S):

WOKE UP AT:
A.M.
P.M.

LAST FED AT:
A.M.
P.M.

MEALS:

	TIME
Breakfast	
Snack	
Lunch	
Snack	
Dinner	

POTTY:

Time	Diaper	Potty	Dry	Wet	BM
	☐	☐	☐	☐	☐
	☐	☐	☐	☐	☐
	☐	☐	☐	☐	☐
	☐	☐	☐	☐	☐
	☐	☐	☐	☐	☐
	☐	☐	☐	☐	☐
	☐	☐	☐	☐	☐

ACTIVITIES:
- [ ] FREE PLAY
- [ ] READING
- [ ] ARTS/CRAFTS
- [ ] MUSIC/SINGING
- [ ] OUTDOORS PLAY
- [ ] TV/MOVIE
- [ ] FIELD TRIP
- [ ] PLAYDATE WITH _____
- [ ] OTHER _____

SLEEP:

FROM	TO

ACCIDENT REPORT:

ACCIDENT	CARE GIVEN

MEDICATION(S):

TIME	TYPE	AMOUNT

SUPPLIES NEEDED:

NOTES TO PARENTS:

TIME IN: **TIME OUT:**

TODDLER REPORT

CHILD'S NAME: _____

DATE: _____

(S) (M) (T) (W) (T) (F) (S)

MOOD:
- ☐ Chatty
- ☐ Happy
- ☐ Cranky
- ☐ Playful
- ☐ Cuddly
- ☐ Quiet
- ☐ Friendly
- ☐ Sad
- ☐ Fussy
- ☐ Sick
- ☐ Grumpy
- ☐ Sleepy
- ☐ Other: _____

NOTES FROM PARENT(S):
_____
_____
_____
_____

WOKE UP AT:
A.M.
P.M.

LAST FED AT:
A.M.
P.M.

MEALS:

	TIME
Breakfast	
Snack	
Lunch	
Snack	
Dinner	

POTTY:

Time	Diaper	Potty	Dry	Wet	BM
___	☐	☐	☐	☐	☐
___	☐	☐	☐	☐	☐
___	☐	☐	☐	☐	☐
___	☐	☐	☐	☐	☐
___	☐	☐	☐	☐	☐
___	☐	☐	☐	☐	☐
___	☐	☐	☐	☐	☐

ACTIVITIES:
- ☐ FREE PLAY
- ☐ READING
- ☐ ARTS/CRAFTS
- ☐ MUSIC/SINGING
- ☐ OUTDOORS PLAY
- ☐ TV/MOVIE
- ☐ FIELD TRIP
- ☐ PLAYDATE WITH _____
- ☐ OTHER _____

SLEEP:

FROM	TO

ACCIDENT REPORT:

ACCIDENT	CARE GIVEN

MEDICATION(S):

TIME	TYPE	AMOUNT

SUPPLIES NEEDED:
_____
_____
_____
_____
_____
_____

NOTES TO PARENTS:
_____
_____
_____
_____
_____

TIME IN: _____   TIME OUT: _____

TODDLER REPORT

CHILD'S NAME:

DATE:

Ⓢ Ⓜ Ⓣ Ⓦ Ⓣ Ⓕ Ⓢ

MOOD:
- ☐ Chatty
- ☐ Happy
- ☐ Cranky
- ☐ Playful
- ☐ Cuddly
- ☐ Quiet
- ☐ Friendly
- ☐ Sad
- ☐ Fussy
- ☐ Sick
- ☐ Grumpy
- ☐ Sleepy
- ☐ Other: _____

NOTES FROM PARENT(S):
_____
_____
_____
_____
_____

WOKE UP AT:
A.M.
P.M.

LAST FED AT:
A.M.
P.M.

MEALS:

	TIME
Breakfast	
Snack	
Lunch	
Snack	
Dinner	

POTTY:

Time	Diaper	Potty	Dry	Wet	BM
____	☐	☐	☐	☐	☐
____	☐	☐	☐	☐	☐
____	☐	☐	☐	☐	☐
____	☐	☐	☐	☐	☐
____	☐	☐	☐	☐	☐
____	☐	☐	☐	☐	☐
____	☐	☐	☐	☐	☐

ACTIVITIES:
- ☐ FREE PLAY
- ☐ READING
- ☐ ARTS/CRAFTS
- ☐ MUSIC/SINGING
- ☐ OUTDOORS PLAY
- ☐ TV/MOVIE
- ☐ FIELD TRIP
- ☐ PLAYDATE WITH _____
- ☐ OTHER _____

SLEEP:

FROM	TO

ACCIDENT REPORT:

ACCIDENT	CARE GIVEN

MEDICATION(S):

TIME	TYPE	AMOUNT

SUPPLIES NEEDED:
_____
_____
_____
_____

NOTES TO PARENTS:
_____
_____
_____
_____
_____

TIME IN: **TIME OUT:**

TODDLER REPORT

DATE:

CHILD'S NAME:

S M T W T F S

MOOD:
- [ ] Chatty
- [ ] Cranky
- [ ] Cuddly
- [ ] Friendly
- [ ] Fussy
- [ ] Grumpy
- [ ] Happy
- [ ] Playful
- [ ] Quiet
- [ ] Sad
- [ ] Sick
- [ ] Sleepy
- [ ] Other: _____

NOTES FROM PARENT(S):

WOKE UP AT:
A.M.
P.M.

LAST FED AT:
A.M.
P.M.

MEALS:

	TIME
Breakfast	
Snack	
Lunch	
Snack	
Dinner	

POTTY:

Time	Diaper	Potty	Dry	Wet	BM
___	☐	☐	☐	☐	☐
___	☐	☐	☐	☐	☐
___	☐	☐	☐	☐	☐
___	☐	☐	☐	☐	☐
___	☐	☐	☐	☐	☐
___	☐	☐	☐	☐	☐
___	☐	☐	☐	☐	☐

ACTIVITIES:
- [ ] FREE PLAY
- [ ] READING
- [ ] ARTS/CRAFTS
- [ ] MUSIC/SINGING
- [ ] OUTDOORS PLAY
- [ ] TV/MOVIE
- [ ] FIELD TRIP
- [ ] PLAYDATE WITH _____
- [ ] OTHER _____

SLEEP:

FROM	TO

ACCIDENT REPORT:

ACCIDENT	CARE GIVEN

MEDICATION(S):

TIME	TYPE	AMOUNT

SUPPLIES NEEDED:

NOTES TO PARENTS:

TIME IN: **TIME OUT:**

TODDLER REPORT

CHILD'S NAME:

DATE:

Ⓢ Ⓜ Ⓣ Ⓦ Ⓣ Ⓕ Ⓢ

MOOD:
- ☐ Chatty
- ☐ Happy
- ☐ Cranky
- ☐ Playful
- ☐ Cuddly
- ☐ Quiet
- ☐ Friendly
- ☐ Sad
- ☐ Fussy
- ☐ Sick
- ☐ Grumpy
- ☐ Sleepy
- ☐ Other: _____

NOTES FROM PARENT(S):
_____
_____
_____
_____
_____

WOKE UP AT:
A.M.
P.M.

LAST FED AT:
A.M.
P.M.

MEALS:

	TIME
Breakfast	
Snack	
Lunch	
Snack	
Dinner	

POTTY:

Time	Diaper	Potty	Dry	Wet	BM
___	☐	☐	☐	☐	☐
___	☐	☐	☐	☐	☐
___	☐	☐	☐	☐	☐
___	☐	☐	☐	☐	☐
___	☐	☐	☐	☐	☐
___	☐	☐	☐	☐	☐
___	☐	☐	☐	☐	☐

ACTIVITIES:
- ☐ FREE PLAY
- ☐ READING
- ☐ ARTS/CRAFTS
- ☐ MUSIC/SINGING
- ☐ OUTDOORS PLAY
- ☐ TV/MOVIE
- ☐ FIELD TRIP
- ☐ PLAYDATE WITH _____
- ☐ OTHER _____

SLEEP:

FROM	TO

ACCIDENT REPORT:

ACCIDENT	CARE GIVEN

MEDICATION(S):

TIME	TYPE	AMOUNT

SUPPLIES NEEDED:
_____
_____
_____
_____
_____

NOTES TO PARENTS:
_____
_____
_____
_____
_____
_____

TIME IN: **TIME OUT:**

TODDLER REPORT

DATE: _____

CHILD'S NAME: _____

(S) (M) (T) (W) (T) (F) (S)

MOOD:
- ☐ Chatty
- ☐ Happy
- ☐ Cranky
- ☐ Playful
- ☐ Cuddly
- ☐ Quiet
- ☐ Friendly
- ☐ Sad
- ☐ Fussy
- ☐ Sick
- ☐ Grumpy
- ☐ Sleepy
- ☐ Other: _____

NOTES FROM PARENT(S):
_____
_____
_____
_____

WOKE UP AT:
_____ A.M.
P.M.

LAST FED AT:
_____ A.M.
P.M.

MEALS:

	TIME
Breakfast	
Snack	
Lunch	
Snack	
Dinner	

POTTY:

Time	Diaper	Potty	Dry	Wet	BM
____	☐	☐	☐	☐	☐
____	☐	☐	☐	☐	☐
____	☐	☐	☐	☐	☐
____	☐	☐	☐	☐	☐
____	☐	☐	☐	☐	☐
____	☐	☐	☐	☐	☐
____	☐	☐	☐	☐	☐

ACTIVITIES:
- ☐ FREE PLAY
- ☐ READING
- ☐ ARTS/CRAFTS
- ☐ MUSIC/SINGING
- ☐ OUTDOORS PLAY
- ☐ TV/MOVIE
- ☐ FIELD TRIP
- ☐ PLAYDATE WITH _____
- ☐ OTHER _____

SLEEP:

FROM	TO

ACCIDENT REPORT:

ACCIDENT	CARE GIVEN

MEDICATION(S):

TIME	TYPE	AMOUNT

SUPPLIES NEEDED:
_____
_____
_____
_____
_____
_____

NOTES TO PARENTS:
_____
_____
_____
_____
_____
_____

TIME IN: _____   TIME OUT: _____

TODDLER REPORT

CHILD'S NAME:

DATE:

Ⓢ Ⓜ Ⓣ Ⓦ Ⓣ Ⓕ Ⓢ

MOOD:
- ☐ Chatty
- ☐ Happy
- ☐ Cranky
- ☐ Playful
- ☐ Cuddly
- ☐ Quiet
- ☐ Friendly
- ☐ Sad
- ☐ Fussy
- ☐ Sick
- ☐ Grumpy
- ☐ Sleepy
- ☐ Other: _____

NOTES FROM PARENT(S):
_____
_____
_____
_____
_____

WOKE UP AT:
A.M.
P.M.

LAST FED AT:
A.M.
P.M.

MEALS:

	TIME
Breakfast	
Snack	
Lunch	
Snack	
Dinner	

POTTY:

Time	Diaper	Potty	Dry	Wet	BM
___	☐	☐	☐	☐	☐
___	☐	☐	☐	☐	☐
___	☐	☐	☐	☐	☐
___	☐	☐	☐	☐	☐
___	☐	☐	☐	☐	☐
___	☐	☐	☐	☐	☐
___	☐	☐	☐	☐	☐

ACTIVITIES:
- ☐ FREE PLAY
- ☐ READING
- ☐ ARTS/CRAFTS
- ☐ MUSIC/SINGING
- ☐ OUTDOORS PLAY
- ☐ TV/MOVIE
- ☐ FIELD TRIP
- ☐ PLAYDATE WITH _____
- ☐ OTHER _____

SLEEP:

FROM	TO

ACCIDENT REPORT:

ACCIDENT	CARE GIVEN

MEDICATION(S):

TIME	TYPE	AMOUNT

SUPPLIES NEEDED:
_____
_____
_____
_____

NOTES TO PARENTS:
_____
_____
_____
_____

TIME IN: **TIME OUT:**

TODDLER REPORT

CHILD'S NAME:

DATE:

Ⓢ Ⓜ Ⓣ Ⓦ Ⓣ Ⓕ Ⓢ

MOOD:
- ☐ Chatty
- ☐ Happy
- ☐ Cranky
- ☐ Playful
- ☐ Cuddly
- ☐ Quiet
- ☐ Friendly
- ☐ Sad
- ☐ Fussy
- ☐ Sick
- ☐ Grumpy
- ☐ Sleepy
- ☐ Other: _____

NOTES FROM PARENT(S):

WOKE UP AT:
A.M.
P.M.

LAST FED AT:
A.M.
P.M.

MEALS:

	TIME
Breakfast	
Snack	
Lunch	
Snack	
Dinner	

POTTY:

Time	Diaper	Potty	Dry	Wet	BM
	☐	☐	☐	☐	☐
	☐	☐	☐	☐	☐
	☐	☐	☐	☐	☐
	☐	☐	☐	☐	☐
	☐	☐	☐	☐	☐
	☐	☐	☐	☐	☐
	☐	☐	☐	☐	☐

ACTIVITIES:
- ☐ FREE PLAY
- ☐ READING
- ☐ ARTS/CRAFTS
- ☐ MUSIC/SINGING
- ☐ OUTDOORS PLAY
- ☐ TV/MOVIE
- ☐ FIELD TRIP
- ☐ PLAYDATE WITH _____
- ☐ OTHER _____

SLEEP:

FROM	TO

ACCIDENT REPORT:

ACCIDENT	CARE GIVEN

MEDICATION(S):

TIME	TYPE	AMOUNT

SUPPLIES NEEDED:

NOTES TO PARENTS:

TIME IN: **TIME OUT:**

TODDLER REPORT

CHILD'S NAME: _____

DATE: _____

Ⓢ Ⓜ Ⓣ Ⓦ Ⓣ Ⓕ Ⓢ

MOOD:
- ☐ Chatty
- ☐ Cranky
- ☐ Cuddly
- ☐ Friendly
- ☐ Fussy
- ☐ Grumpy
- ☐ Happy
- ☐ Playful
- ☐ Quiet
- ☐ Sad
- ☐ Sick
- ☐ Sleepy
- ☐ Other: _____

NOTES FROM PARENT(S):
_____
_____
_____
_____
_____

WOKE UP AT:
_____ A.M. / P.M.

LAST FED AT:
_____ A.M. / P.M.

MEALS:

	TIME
Breakfast	
Snack	
Lunch	
Snack	
Dinner	

POTTY:

Time	Diaper	Potty	Dry	Wet	BM
_____	☐	☐	☐	☐	☐
_____	☐	☐	☐	☐	☐
_____	☐	☐	☐	☐	☐
_____	☐	☐	☐	☐	☐
_____	☐	☐	☐	☐	☐
_____	☐	☐	☐	☐	☐
_____	☐	☐	☐	☐	☐

ACTIVITIES:
- ☐ FREE PLAY
- ☐ READING
- ☐ ARTS/CRAFTS
- ☐ MUSIC/SINGING
- ☐ OUTDOORS PLAY
- ☐ TV/MOVIE
- ☐ FIELD TRIP
- ☐ PLAYDATE WITH _____
- ☐ OTHER _____

SLEEP:

FROM	TO

ACCIDENT REPORT:

ACCIDENT	CARE GIVEN

MEDICATION(S):

TIME	TYPE	AMOUNT

SUPPLIES NEEDED:
_____
_____
_____
_____
_____

NOTES TO PARENTS:
_____
_____
_____
_____
_____

TIME IN: _____   TIME OUT: _____

TODDLER REPORT

CHILD'S NAME: _____

DATE: _____

Ⓢ Ⓜ Ⓣ Ⓦ Ⓣ Ⓕ Ⓢ

MOOD:
- ☐ Chatty
- ☐ Happy
- ☐ Cranky
- ☐ Playful
- ☐ Cuddly
- ☐ Quiet
- ☐ Friendly
- ☐ Sad
- ☐ Fussy
- ☐ Sick
- ☐ Grumpy
- ☐ Sleepy
- ☐ Other: _____

NOTES FROM PARENT(S):
_____
_____
_____
_____

WOKE UP AT:
_____
A.M.
P.M.

LAST FED AT:
_____
A.M.
P.M.

MEALS:

	TIME
Breakfast	
Snack	
Lunch	
Snack	
Dinner	

POTTY:

Time	Diaper	Potty	Dry	Wet	BM
____	☐	☐	☐	☐	☐
____	☐	☐	☐	☐	☐
____	☐	☐	☐	☐	☐
____	☐	☐	☐	☐	☐
____	☐	☐	☐	☐	☐
____	☐	☐	☐	☐	☐
____	☐	☐	☐	☐	☐

ACTIVITIES:
- ☐ FREE PLAY
- ☐ READING
- ☐ ARTS/CRAFTS
- ☐ MUSIC/SINGING
- ☐ OUTDOORS PLAY
- ☐ TV/MOVIE
- ☐ FIELD TRIP
- ☐ PLAYDATE WITH _____
- ☐ OTHER _____

SLEEP:

FROM	TO

ACCIDENT REPORT:

ACCIDENT	CARE GIVEN

MEDICATION(S):

TIME	TYPE	AMOUNT

SUPPLIES NEEDED:
_____
_____
_____
_____
_____
_____

NOTES TO PARENTS:
_____
_____
_____
_____
_____
_____

TIME IN: _____ **TIME OUT:** _____

TODDLER REPORT

CHILD'S NAME:

DATE:

(S) (M) (T) (W) (T) (F) (S)

MOOD:
- ☐ Chatty
- ☐ Happy
- ☐ Cranky
- ☐ Playful
- ☐ Cuddly
- ☐ Quiet
- ☐ Friendly
- ☐ Sad
- ☐ Fussy
- ☐ Sick
- ☐ Grumpy
- ☐ Sleepy
- ☐ Other: _____

NOTES FROM PARENT(S):
_____
_____
_____
_____
_____

WOKE UP AT:
A.M.
P.M.

LAST FED AT:
A.M.
P.M.

MEALS:

	TIME
Breakfast	
Snack	
Lunch	
Snack	
Dinner	

POTTY:

Time	Diaper	Potty	Dry	Wet	BM
___	☐	☐	☐	☐	☐
___	☐	☐	☐	☐	☐
___	☐	☐	☐	☐	☐
___	☐	☐	☐	☐	☐
___	☐	☐	☐	☐	☐
___	☐	☐	☐	☐	☐
___	☐	☐	☐	☐	☐

ACTIVITIES:
- ☐ FREE PLAY
- ☐ READING
- ☐ ARTS/CRAFTS
- ☐ MUSIC/SINGING
- ☐ OUTDOORS PLAY
- ☐ TV/MOVIE
- ☐ FIELD TRIP
- ☐ PLAYDATE WITH _____
- ☐ OTHER _____

SLEEP:

FROM	TO

ACCIDENT REPORT:

ACCIDENT	CARE GIVEN

MEDICATION(S):

TIME	TYPE	AMOUNT

SUPPLIES NEEDED:
_____
_____
_____
_____
_____

NOTES TO PARENTS:
_____
_____
_____
_____
_____

TIME IN: **TIME OUT:**

TODDLER REPORT

CHILD'S NAME:

DATE:

Ⓢ Ⓜ Ⓣ Ⓦ Ⓣ Ⓕ Ⓢ

MOOD:
- ☐ Chatty
- ☐ Happy
- ☐ Cranky
- ☐ Playful
- ☐ Cuddly
- ☐ Quiet
- ☐ Friendly
- ☐ Sad
- ☐ Fussy
- ☐ Sick
- ☐ Grumpy
- ☐ Sleepy
- ☐ Other: _____

NOTES FROM PARENT(S):

WOKE UP AT:
A.M.
P.M.

LAST FED AT:
A.M.
P.M.

MEALS:

	TIME
Breakfast	
Snack	
Lunch	
Snack	
Dinner	

POTTY:

Time	Diaper	Potty	Dry	Wet	BM
	☐	☐	☐	☐	☐
	☐	☐	☐	☐	☐
	☐	☐	☐	☐	☐
	☐	☐	☐	☐	☐
	☐	☐	☐	☐	☐
	☐	☐	☐	☐	☐
	☐	☐	☐	☐	☐

ACTIVITIES:
- ☐ FREE PLAY
- ☐ READING
- ☐ ARTS/CRAFTS
- ☐ MUSIC/SINGING
- ☐ OUTDOORS PLAY
- ☐ TV/MOVIE
- ☐ FIELD TRIP
- ☐ PLAYDATE WITH _____
- ☐ OTHER _____

SLEEP:

FROM	TO

ACCIDENT REPORT:

ACCIDENT	CARE GIVEN

MEDICATION(S):

TIME	TYPE	AMOUNT

SUPPLIES NEEDED:

NOTES TO PARENTS:

TIME IN: **TIME OUT:**

TODDLER REPORT

CHILD'S NAME:

DATE:

Ⓢ Ⓜ Ⓣ Ⓦ Ⓣ Ⓕ Ⓢ

MOOD:
- ☐ Chatty
- ☐ Happy
- ☐ Cranky
- ☐ Playful
- ☐ Cuddly
- ☐ Quiet
- ☐ Friendly
- ☐ Sad
- ☐ Fussy
- ☐ Sick
- ☐ Grumpy
- ☐ Sleepy
- ☐ Other: _____

NOTES FROM PARENT(S):

WOKE UP AT:
A.M.
P.M.

LAST FED AT:
A.M.
P.M.

MEALS:
	TIME
Breakfast	
Snack	
Lunch	
Snack	
Dinner	

POTTY:
Time	Diaper	Potty	Dry	Wet	BM
	☐	☐	☐	☐	☐
	☐	☐	☐	☐	☐
	☐	☐	☐	☐	☐
	☐	☐	☐	☐	☐
	☐	☐	☐	☐	☐
	☐	☐	☐	☐	☐
	☐	☐	☐	☐	☐

ACTIVITIES:
- ☐ FREE PLAY
- ☐ READING
- ☐ ARTS/CRAFTS
- ☐ MUSIC/SINGING
- ☐ OUTDOORS PLAY
- ☐ TV/MOVIE
- ☐ FIELD TRIP
- ☐ PLAYDATE WITH _____
- ☐ OTHER _____

SLEEP:
FROM	TO

ACCIDENT REPORT:
ACCIDENT	CARE GIVEN

MEDICATION(S):
TIME	TYPE	AMOUNT

SUPPLIES NEEDED:

NOTES TO PARENTS:

TIME IN: **TIME OUT:**

TODDLER REPORT

CHILD'S NAME:

DATE:

(S) (M) (T) (W) (T) (F) (S)

MOOD:
- ☐ Chatty
- ☐ Happy
- ☐ Cranky
- ☐ Playful
- ☐ Cuddly
- ☐ Quiet
- ☐ Friendly
- ☐ Sad
- ☐ Fussy
- ☐ Sick
- ☐ Grumpy
- ☐ Sleepy
- ☐ Other: _____

NOTES FROM PARENT(S):
_____
_____
_____
_____

WOKE UP AT:
A.M.
P.M.

LAST FED AT:
A.M.
P.M.

MEALS:

	TIME
Breakfast	
Snack	
Lunch	
Snack	
Dinner	

POTTY:

Time	Diaper	Potty	Dry	Wet	BM
	☐	☐	☐	☐	☐
	☐	☐	☐	☐	☐
	☐	☐	☐	☐	☐
	☐	☐	☐	☐	☐
	☐	☐	☐	☐	☐
	☐	☐	☐	☐	☐
	☐	☐	☐	☐	☐

ACTIVITIES:
- ☐ FREE PLAY
- ☐ READING
- ☐ ARTS/CRAFTS
- ☐ MUSIC/SINGING
- ☐ OUTDOORS PLAY
- ☐ TV/MOVIE
- ☐ FIELD TRIP
- ☐ PLAYDATE WITH _____
- ☐ OTHER _____

SLEEP:

FROM	TO

ACCIDENT REPORT:

ACCIDENT	CARE GIVEN

MEDICATION(S):

TIME	TYPE	AMOUNT

SUPPLIES NEEDED:
_____
_____
_____
_____
_____

NOTES TO PARENTS:
_____
_____
_____
_____
_____

TIME IN: **TIME OUT:**

TODDLER REPORT

CHILD'S NAME: _____

DATE: _____

Ⓢ Ⓜ Ⓣ Ⓦ Ⓣ Ⓕ Ⓢ

MOOD:
- ☐ Chatty
- ☐ Cranky
- ☐ Cuddly
- ☐ Friendly
- ☐ Fussy
- ☐ Grumpy
- ☐ Happy
- ☐ Playful
- ☐ Quiet
- ☐ Sad
- ☐ Sick
- ☐ Sleepy
- ☐ Other: _____

NOTES FROM PARENT(S):
_____
_____
_____
_____
_____

WOKE UP AT:
A.M.
P.M.

LAST FED AT:
A.M.
P.M.

MEALS:

	TIME
Breakfast	
Snack	
Lunch	
Snack	
Dinner	

POTTY:

Time	Diaper	Potty	Dry	Wet	BM
_____	☐	☐	☐	☐	☐
_____	☐	☐	☐	☐	☐
_____	☐	☐	☐	☐	☐
_____	☐	☐	☐	☐	☐
_____	☐	☐	☐	☐	☐
_____	☐	☐	☐	☐	☐
_____	☐	☐	☐	☐	☐

ACTIVITIES:
- ☐ FREE PLAY
- ☐ READING
- ☐ ARTS/CRAFTS
- ☐ MUSIC/SINGING
- ☐ OUTDOORS PLAY
- ☐ TV/MOVIE
- ☐ FIELD TRIP
- ☐ PLAYDATE WITH _____
- ☐ OTHER _____

SLEEP:

FROM	TO

ACCIDENT REPORT:

ACCIDENT	CARE GIVEN

MEDICATION(S):

TIME	TYPE	AMOUNT

SUPPLIES NEEDED:
_____
_____
_____
_____
_____

NOTES TO PARENTS:
_____
_____
_____
_____
_____

TIME IN: _____   TIME OUT: _____

TODDLER REPORT

CHILD'S NAME:

DATE:

S M T W T F S

MOOD:
- ☐ Chatty
- ☐ Cranky
- ☐ Cuddly
- ☐ Friendly
- ☐ Fussy
- ☐ Grumpy
- ☐ Happy
- ☐ Playful
- ☐ Quiet
- ☐ Sad
- ☐ Sick
- ☐ Sleepy
- ☐ Other: _____

NOTES FROM PARENT(S):

WOKE UP AT:
A.M.
P.M.

LAST FED AT:
A.M.
P.M.

MEALS:

	TIME
Breakfast	
Snack	
Lunch	
Snack	
Dinner	

POTTY:

Time	Diaper	Potty	Dry	Wet	BM
	☐	☐	☐	☐	☐
	☐	☐	☐	☐	☐
	☐	☐	☐	☐	☐
	☐	☐	☐	☐	☐
	☐	☐	☐	☐	☐
	☐	☐	☐	☐	☐
	☐	☐	☐	☐	☐

ACTIVITIES:
- ☐ FREE PLAY
- ☐ READING
- ☐ ARTS/CRAFTS
- ☐ MUSIC/SINGING
- ☐ OUTDOORS PLAY
- ☐ TV/MOVIE
- ☐ FIELD TRIP
- ☐ PLAYDATE WITH _____
- ☐ OTHER _____

SLEEP:

FROM	TO

ACCIDENT REPORT:

ACCIDENT	CARE GIVEN

MEDICATION(S):

TIME	TYPE	AMOUNT

SUPPLIES NEEDED:

NOTES TO PARENTS:

TIME IN: **TIME OUT:**

TODDLER REPORT

CHILD'S NAME:

DATE:

Ⓢ Ⓜ Ⓣ Ⓦ Ⓣ Ⓕ Ⓢ

MOOD:
- ☐ Chatty
- ☐ Cranky
- ☐ Cuddly
- ☐ Friendly
- ☐ Fussy
- ☐ Grumpy
- ☐ Happy
- ☐ Playful
- ☐ Quiet
- ☐ Sad
- ☐ Sick
- ☐ Sleepy
- ☐ Other: _____

NOTES FROM PARENT(S):
_____
_____
_____
_____

WOKE UP AT:
A.M.
P.M.

LAST FED AT:
A.M.
P.M.

MEALS:

	TIME
Breakfast	
Snack	
Lunch	
Snack	
Dinner	

POTTY:

Time	Diaper	Potty	Dry	Wet	BM
___	☐	☐	☐	☐	☐
___	☐	☐	☐	☐	☐
___	☐	☐	☐	☐	☐
___	☐	☐	☐	☐	☐
___	☐	☐	☐	☐	☐
___	☐	☐	☐	☐	☐
___	☐	☐	☐	☐	☐

ACTIVITIES:
- ☐ FREE PLAY
- ☐ READING
- ☐ ARTS/CRAFTS
- ☐ MUSIC/SINGING
- ☐ OUTDOORS PLAY
- ☐ TV/MOVIE
- ☐ FIELD TRIP
- ☐ PLAYDATE WITH _____
- ☐ OTHER _____

SLEEP:

FROM	TO

ACCIDENT REPORT:

ACCIDENT	CARE GIVEN

MEDICATION(S):

TIME	TYPE	AMOUNT

SUPPLIES NEEDED:
_____
_____
_____
_____

NOTES TO PARENTS:
_____
_____
_____
_____
_____

TIME IN: **TIME OUT:**

TODDLER REPORT

CHILD'S NAME:

DATE:

S M T W T F S

MOOD:
- ☐ Chatty
- ☐ Happy
- ☐ Cranky
- ☐ Playful
- ☐ Cuddly
- ☐ Quiet
- ☐ Friendly
- ☐ Sad
- ☐ Fussy
- ☐ Sick
- ☐ Grumpy
- ☐ Sleepy
- ☐ Other: _____

NOTES FROM PARENT(S):
_____
_____
_____
_____
_____

WOKE UP AT:
A.M.
P.M.

LAST FED AT:
A.M.
P.M.

MEALS:

	TIME
Breakfast	
Snack	
Lunch	
Snack	
Dinner	

POTTY:

Time	Diaper	Potty	Dry	Wet	BM
___	☐	☐	☐	☐	☐
___	☐	☐	☐	☐	☐
___	☐	☐	☐	☐	☐
___	☐	☐	☐	☐	☐
___	☐	☐	☐	☐	☐
___	☐	☐	☐	☐	☐
___	☐	☐	☐	☐	☐

ACTIVITIES:
- ☐ FREE PLAY
- ☐ READING
- ☐ ARTS/CRAFTS
- ☐ MUSIC/SINGING
- ☐ OUTDOORS PLAY
- ☐ TV/MOVIE
- ☐ FIELD TRIP
- ☐ PLAYDATE WITH _____
- ☐ OTHER _____

SLEEP:

FROM	TO

ACCIDENT REPORT:

ACCIDENT	CARE GIVEN

MEDICATION(S):

TIME	TYPE	AMOUNT

SUPPLIES NEEDED:
_____
_____
_____
_____
_____
_____

NOTES TO PARENTS:
_____
_____
_____
_____
_____

TIME IN: TIME OUT:

TODDLER REPORT

CHILD'S NAME:

DATE:

Ⓢ Ⓜ Ⓣ Ⓦ Ⓣ Ⓕ Ⓢ

MOOD:
- ☐ Chatty
- ☐ Happy
- ☐ Cranky
- ☐ Playful
- ☐ Cuddly
- ☐ Quiet
- ☐ Friendly
- ☐ Sad
- ☐ Fussy
- ☐ Sick
- ☐ Grumpy
- ☐ Sleepy
- ☐ Other: _____

NOTES FROM PARENT(S):
_____
_____
_____
_____

WOKE UP AT:
A.M.
P.M.

LAST FED AT:
A.M.
P.M.

MEALS:

	TIME
Breakfast	
Snack	
Lunch	
Snack	
Dinner	

POTTY:

Time	Diaper	Potty	Dry	Wet	BM
	☐	☐	☐	☐	☐
	☐	☐	☐	☐	☐
	☐	☐	☐	☐	☐
	☐	☐	☐	☐	☐
	☐	☐	☐	☐	☐
	☐	☐	☐	☐	☐
	☐	☐	☐	☐	☐

ACTIVITIES:
- ☐ FREE PLAY
- ☐ READING
- ☐ ARTS/CRAFTS
- ☐ MUSIC/SINGING
- ☐ OUTDOORS PLAY
- ☐ TV/MOVIE
- ☐ FIELD TRIP
- ☐ PLAYDATE WITH _____
- ☐ OTHER _____

SLEEP:

FROM	TO

ACCIDENT REPORT:

ACCIDENT	CARE GIVEN

MEDICATION(S):

TIME	TYPE	AMOUNT

SUPPLIES NEEDED:
_____
_____
_____
_____
_____

NOTES TO PARENTS:
_____
_____
_____
_____
_____

TIME IN: **TIME OUT:**

TODDLER REPORT

CHILD'S NAME: _____

DATE: _____

Ⓢ Ⓜ Ⓣ Ⓦ Ⓣ Ⓕ Ⓢ

MOOD:
- ☐ Chatty
- ☐ Cranky
- ☐ Cuddly
- ☐ Friendly
- ☐ Fussy
- ☐ Grumpy
- ☐ Happy
- ☐ Playful
- ☐ Quiet
- ☐ Sad
- ☐ Sick
- ☐ Sleepy
- ☐ Other: _____

NOTES FROM PARENT(S):
_____
_____
_____
_____
_____

WOKE UP AT:
_____ A.M. / P.M.

LAST FED AT:
_____ A.M. / P.M.

MEALS:

	TIME
Breakfast	
Snack	
Lunch	
Snack	
Dinner	

POTTY:

Time	Diaper	Potty	Dry	Wet	BM
_____	☐	☐	☐	☐	☐
_____	☐	☐	☐	☐	☐
_____	☐	☐	☐	☐	☐
_____	☐	☐	☐	☐	☐
_____	☐	☐	☐	☐	☐
_____	☐	☐	☐	☐	☐
_____	☐	☐	☐	☐	☐

ACTIVITIES:
- ☐ FREE PLAY
- ☐ READING
- ☐ ARTS/CRAFTS
- ☐ MUSIC/SINGING
- ☐ OUTDOORS PLAY
- ☐ TV/MOVIE
- ☐ FIELD TRIP
- ☐ PLAYDATE WITH _____
- ☐ OTHER _____

SLEEP:

FROM	TO

ACCIDENT REPORT:

ACCIDENT	CARE GIVEN

MEDICATION(S):

TIME	TYPE	AMOUNT

SUPPLIES NEEDED:
_____
_____
_____
_____
_____
_____

NOTES TO PARENTS:
_____
_____
_____
_____
_____
_____

TIME IN: _____ TIME OUT: _____

TODDLER REPORT

CHILD'S NAME:

DATE:

Ⓢ Ⓜ Ⓣ Ⓦ Ⓣ Ⓕ Ⓢ

MOOD:
- ☐ Chatty
- ☐ Cranky
- ☐ Cuddly
- ☐ Friendly
- ☐ Fussy
- ☐ Grumpy
- ☐ Happy
- ☐ Playful
- ☐ Quiet
- ☐ Sad
- ☐ Sick
- ☐ Sleepy
- ☐ Other: _____

NOTES FROM PARENT(S):
_____
_____
_____
_____
_____

WOKE UP AT:
A.M.
P.M.

LAST FED AT:
A.M.
P.M.

MEALS:

	TIME
Breakfast	
Snack	
Lunch	
Snack	
Dinner	

POTTY:

Time	Diaper	Potty	Dry	Wet	BM
____	☐	☐	☐	☐	☐
____	☐	☐	☐	☐	☐
____	☐	☐	☐	☐	☐
____	☐	☐	☐	☐	☐
____	☐	☐	☐	☐	☐
____	☐	☐	☐	☐	☐
____	☐	☐	☐	☐	☐

ACTIVITIES:
- ☐ FREE PLAY
- ☐ READING
- ☐ ARTS/CRAFTS
- ☐ MUSIC/SINGING
- ☐ OUTDOORS PLAY
- ☐ TV/MOVIE
- ☐ FIELD TRIP
- ☐ PLAYDATE WITH _____
- ☐ OTHER _____

SLEEP:

FROM	TO

ACCIDENT REPORT:

ACCIDENT	CARE GIVEN

MEDICATION(S):

TIME	TYPE	AMOUNT

SUPPLIES NEEDED:
_____
_____
_____
_____
_____

NOTES TO PARENTS:
_____
_____
_____
_____
_____
_____

TIME IN: **TIME OUT:**

TODDLER REPORT

CHILD'S NAME: _____

DATE: _____

Ⓢ Ⓜ Ⓣ Ⓦ Ⓣ Ⓕ Ⓢ

MOOD:
- ☐ Chatty
- ☐ Happy
- ☐ Cranky
- ☐ Playful
- ☐ Cuddly
- ☐ Quiet
- ☐ Friendly
- ☐ Sad
- ☐ Fussy
- ☐ Sick
- ☐ Grumpy
- ☐ Sleepy
- ☐ Other: _____

NOTES FROM PARENT(S):
_____
_____
_____
_____
_____

WOKE UP AT:
_____ A.M.
P.M.

LAST FED AT:
_____ A.M.
P.M.

MEALS:

	TIME
Breakfast	
Snack	
Lunch	
Snack	
Dinner	

POTTY:

Time	Diaper	Potty	Dry	Wet	BM
____	☐	☐	☐	☐	☐
____	☐	☐	☐	☐	☐
____	☐	☐	☐	☐	☐
____	☐	☐	☐	☐	☐
____	☐	☐	☐	☐	☐
____	☐	☐	☐	☐	☐
____	☐	☐	☐	☐	☐

ACTIVITIES:
- ☐ FREE PLAY
- ☐ READING
- ☐ ARTS/CRAFTS
- ☐ MUSIC/SINGING
- ☐ OUTDOORS PLAY
- ☐ TV/MOVIE
- ☐ FIELD TRIP
- ☐ PLAYDATE WITH _____
- ☐ OTHER _____

SLEEP:

FROM	TO

ACCIDENT REPORT:

ACCIDENT	CARE GIVEN

MEDICATION(S):

TIME	TYPE	AMOUNT

SUPPLIES NEEDED:
_____
_____
_____
_____
_____

NOTES TO PARENTS:
_____
_____
_____
_____
_____

TIME IN: _____ TIME OUT: _____

TODDLER REPORT

CHILD'S NAME:

DATE:

Ⓢ Ⓜ Ⓣ Ⓦ Ⓣ Ⓕ Ⓢ

MOOD:
- ☐ Chatty
- ☐ Cranky
- ☐ Cuddly
- ☐ Friendly
- ☐ Fussy
- ☐ Grumpy
- ☐ Happy
- ☐ Playful
- ☐ Quiet
- ☐ Sad
- ☐ Sick
- ☐ Sleepy
- ☐ Other: _____

NOTES FROM PARENT(S):

WOKE UP AT:
A.M.
P.M.

LAST FED AT:
A.M.
P.M.

MEALS:

	TIME
Breakfast	
Snack	
Lunch	
Snack	
Dinner	

POTTY:

Time	Diaper	Potty	Dry	Wet	BM
	☐	☐	☐	☐	☐
	☐	☐	☐	☐	☐
	☐	☐	☐	☐	☐
	☐	☐	☐	☐	☐
	☐	☐	☐	☐	☐
	☐	☐	☐	☐	☐
	☐	☐	☐	☐	☐

ACTIVITIES:
- ☐ FREE PLAY
- ☐ READING
- ☐ ARTS/CRAFTS
- ☐ MUSIC/SINGING
- ☐ OUTDOORS PLAY
- ☐ TV/MOVIE
- ☐ FIELD TRIP
- ☐ PLAYDATE WITH _____
- ☐ OTHER _____

SLEEP:

FROM	TO

ACCIDENT REPORT:

ACCIDENT	CARE GIVEN

MEDICATION(S):

TIME	TYPE	AMOUNT

SUPPLIES NEEDED:

NOTES TO PARENTS:

TIME IN: TIME OUT:

TODDLER REPORT

DATE:

CHILD'S NAME:

Ⓢ Ⓜ Ⓣ Ⓦ Ⓣ Ⓕ Ⓢ

MOOD:
- ☐ Chatty
- ☐ Happy
- ☐ Cranky
- ☐ Playful
- ☐ Cuddly
- ☐ Quiet
- ☐ Friendly
- ☐ Sad
- ☐ Fussy
- ☐ Sick
- ☐ Grumpy
- ☐ Sleepy
- ☐ Other: _____

NOTES FROM PARENT(S):

WOKE UP AT:
A.M.
P.M.

LAST FED AT:
A.M.
P.M.

MEALS:

	TIME
Breakfast	
Snack	
Lunch	
Snack	
Dinner	

POTTY:

Time	Diaper	Potty	Dry	Wet	BM
	☐	☐	☐	☐	☐
	☐	☐	☐	☐	☐
	☐	☐	☐	☐	☐
	☐	☐	☐	☐	☐
	☐	☐	☐	☐	☐
	☐	☐	☐	☐	☐
	☐	☐	☐	☐	☐

ACTIVITIES:
- ☐ FREE PLAY
- ☐ READING
- ☐ ARTS/CRAFTS
- ☐ MUSIC/SINGING
- ☐ OUTDOORS PLAY
- ☐ TV/MOVIE
- ☐ FIELD TRIP
- ☐ PLAYDATE WITH _____
- ☐ OTHER _____

SLEEP:

FROM	TO

ACCIDENT REPORT:

ACCIDENT	CARE GIVEN

MEDICATION(S):

TIME	TYPE	AMOUNT

SUPPLIES NEEDED:

NOTES TO PARENTS:

TIME IN: TIME OUT:

TODDLER REPORT

CHILD'S NAME:

DATE:

Ⓢ Ⓜ Ⓣ Ⓦ Ⓣ Ⓕ Ⓢ

MOOD:
- ☐ Chatty
- ☐ Cranky
- ☐ Cuddly
- ☐ Friendly
- ☐ Fussy
- ☐ Grumpy
- ☐ Happy
- ☐ Playful
- ☐ Quiet
- ☐ Sad
- ☐ Sick
- ☐ Sleepy
- ☐ Other: _____

NOTES FROM PARENT(S):

WOKE UP AT:
A.M.
P.M.

LAST FED AT:
A.M.
P.M.

MEALS:

	TIME
Breakfast	
Snack	
Lunch	
Snack	
Dinner	

POTTY:

Time	Diaper	Potty	Dry	Wet	BM
	☐	☐	☐	☐	☐
	☐	☐	☐	☐	☐
	☐	☐	☐	☐	☐
	☐	☐	☐	☐	☐
	☐	☐	☐	☐	☐
	☐	☐	☐	☐	☐
	☐	☐	☐	☐	☐

ACTIVITIES:
- ☐ FREE PLAY
- ☐ READING
- ☐ ARTS/CRAFTS
- ☐ MUSIC/SINGING
- ☐ OUTDOORS PLAY
- ☐ TV/MOVIE
- ☐ FIELD TRIP
- ☐ PLAYDATE WITH _____
- ☐ OTHER _____

SLEEP:

FROM	TO

ACCIDENT REPORT:

ACCIDENT	CARE GIVEN

MEDICATION(S):

TIME	TYPE	AMOUNT

SUPPLIES NEEDED:

NOTES TO PARENTS:

TIME IN: **TIME OUT:**

TODDLER REPORT

DATE:

CHILD'S NAME:

(S) (M) (T) (W) (T) (F) (S)

MOOD:
- ☐ Chatty
- ☐ Happy
- ☐ Cranky
- ☐ Playful
- ☐ Cuddly
- ☐ Quiet
- ☐ Friendly
- ☐ Sad
- ☐ Fussy
- ☐ Sick
- ☐ Grumpy
- ☐ Sleepy
- ☐ Other: _____

NOTES FROM PARENT(S):

WOKE UP AT:
A.M.
P.M.

LAST FED AT:
A.M.
P.M.

MEALS:

	TIME
Breakfast	
Snack	
Lunch	
Snack	
Dinner	

POTTY:

Time	Diaper	Potty	Dry	Wet	BM
	☐	☐	☐	☐	☐
	☐	☐	☐	☐	☐
	☐	☐	☐	☐	☐
	☐	☐	☐	☐	☐
	☐	☐	☐	☐	☐
	☐	☐	☐	☐	☐
	☐	☐	☐	☐	☐

ACTIVITIES:
- ☐ FREE PLAY
- ☐ READING
- ☐ ARTS/CRAFTS
- ☐ MUSIC/SINGING
- ☐ OUTDOORS PLAY
- ☐ TV/MOVIE
- ☐ FIELD TRIP
- ☐ PLAYDATE WITH _____
- ☐ OTHER _____

SLEEP:

FROM	TO

ACCIDENT REPORT:

ACCIDENT	CARE GIVEN

MEDICATION(S):

TIME	TYPE	AMOUNT

SUPPLIES NEEDED:

NOTES TO PARENTS:

TIME IN: TIME OUT:

TODDLER REPORT

CHILD'S NAME:

DATE:

Ⓢ Ⓜ Ⓣ Ⓦ Ⓣ Ⓕ Ⓢ

MOOD:
- ☐ Chatty
- ☐ Cranky
- ☐ Cuddly
- ☐ Friendly
- ☐ Fussy
- ☐ Grumpy
- ☐ Happy
- ☐ Playful
- ☐ Quiet
- ☐ Sad
- ☐ Sick
- ☐ Sleepy
- ☐ Other: _____

NOTES FROM PARENT(S):
_____
_____
_____
_____

WOKE UP AT:
A.M.
P.M.

LAST FED AT:
A.M.
P.M.

MEALS:

	TIME
Breakfast	
Snack	
Lunch	
Snack	
Dinner	

POTTY:

Time	Diaper	Potty	Dry	Wet	BM
____	☐	☐	☐	☐	☐
____	☐	☐	☐	☐	☐
____	☐	☐	☐	☐	☐
____	☐	☐	☐	☐	☐
____	☐	☐	☐	☐	☐
____	☐	☐	☐	☐	☐
____	☐	☐	☐	☐	☐

ACTIVITIES:
- ☐ FREE PLAY
- ☐ READING
- ☐ ARTS/CRAFTS
- ☐ MUSIC/SINGING
- ☐ OUTDOORS PLAY
- ☐ TV/MOVIE
- ☐ FIELD TRIP
- ☐ PLAYDATE WITH _____
- ☐ OTHER _____

SLEEP:

FROM	TO

ACCIDENT REPORT:

ACCIDENT	CARE GIVEN

MEDICATION(S):

TIME	TYPE	AMOUNT

SUPPLIES NEEDED:
_____
_____
_____
_____

NOTES TO PARENTS:
_____
_____
_____
_____
_____

TIME IN:　　　**TIME OUT:**

TODDLER REPORT

CHILD'S NAME:

DATE:

Ⓢ Ⓜ Ⓣ Ⓦ Ⓣ Ⓕ Ⓢ

MOOD:
- ☐ Chatty
- ☐ Cranky
- ☐ Cuddly
- ☐ Friendly
- ☐ Fussy
- ☐ Grumpy
- ☐ Happy
- ☐ Playful
- ☐ Quiet
- ☐ Sad
- ☐ Sick
- ☐ Sleepy
- ☐ Other: _____

NOTES FROM PARENT(S):
_____
_____
_____
_____

WOKE UP AT:
A.M.
P.M.

LAST FED AT:
A.M.
P.M.

MEALS:

	TIME
Breakfast	
Snack	
Lunch	
Snack	
Dinner	

POTTY:

Time	Diaper	Potty	Dry	Wet	BM
	☐	☐	☐	☐	☐
	☐	☐	☐	☐	☐
	☐	☐	☐	☐	☐
	☐	☐	☐	☐	☐
	☐	☐	☐	☐	☐
	☐	☐	☐	☐	☐
	☐	☐	☐	☐	☐

ACTIVITIES:
- ☐ FREE PLAY
- ☐ READING
- ☐ ARTS/CRAFTS
- ☐ MUSIC/SINGING
- ☐ OUTDOORS PLAY
- ☐ TV/MOVIE
- ☐ FIELD TRIP
- ☐ PLAYDATE WITH _____
- ☐ OTHER _____

SLEEP:

FROM	TO

ACCIDENT REPORT:

ACCIDENT	CARE GIVEN

MEDICATION(S):

TIME	TYPE	AMOUNT

SUPPLIES NEEDED:
_____
_____
_____
_____
_____

NOTES TO PARENTS:
_____
_____
_____
_____
_____

TIME IN: **TIME OUT:**

TODDLER REPORT

CHILD'S NAME:

DATE:

S M T W T F S

MOOD:
- ☐ Chatty
- ☐ Happy
- ☐ Cranky
- ☐ Playful
- ☐ Cuddly
- ☐ Quiet
- ☐ Friendly
- ☐ Sad
- ☐ Fussy
- ☐ Sick
- ☐ Grumpy
- ☐ Sleepy
- ☐ Other: _____

NOTES FROM PARENT(S):

WOKE UP AT:
A.M.
P.M.

LAST FED AT:
A.M.
P.M.

MEALS:

	TIME
Breakfast	
Snack	
Lunch	
Snack	
Dinner	

POTTY:

Time	Diaper	Potty	Dry	Wet	BM
____	☐	☐	☐	☐	☐
____	☐	☐	☐	☐	☐
____	☐	☐	☐	☐	☐
____	☐	☐	☐	☐	☐
____	☐	☐	☐	☐	☐
____	☐	☐	☐	☐	☐
____	☐	☐	☐	☐	☐

ACTIVITIES:
- ☐ FREE PLAY
- ☐ READING
- ☐ ARTS/CRAFTS
- ☐ MUSIC/SINGING
- ☐ OUTDOORS PLAY
- ☐ TV/MOVIE
- ☐ FIELD TRIP
- ☐ PLAYDATE WITH _____
- ☐ OTHER _____

SLEEP:

FROM	TO

ACCIDENT REPORT:

ACCIDENT	CARE GIVEN

MEDICATION(S):

TIME	TYPE	AMOUNT

SUPPLIES NEEDED:

NOTES TO PARENTS:

TIME IN: **TIME OUT:**

TODDLER REPORT

CHILD'S NAME:

DATE:

(S) (M) (T) (W) (T) (F) (S)

MOOD:
- ☐ Chatty
- ☐ Happy
- ☐ Cranky
- ☐ Playful
- ☐ Cuddly
- ☐ Quiet
- ☐ Friendly
- ☐ Sad
- ☐ Fussy
- ☐ Sick
- ☐ Grumpy
- ☐ Sleepy
- ☐ Other: _____

NOTES FROM PARENT(S):
_____
_____
_____
_____

WOKE UP AT:
A.M.
P.M.

LAST FED AT:
A.M.
P.M.

MEALS:

	TIME
Breakfast	
Snack	
Lunch	
Snack	
Dinner	

POTTY:

Time	Diaper	Potty	Dry	Wet	BM
___	☐	☐	☐	☐	☐
___	☐	☐	☐	☐	☐
___	☐	☐	☐	☐	☐
___	☐	☐	☐	☐	☐
___	☐	☐	☐	☐	☐
___	☐	☐	☐	☐	☐
___	☐	☐	☐	☐	☐

ACTIVITIES:
- ☐ FREE PLAY
- ☐ READING
- ☐ ARTS/CRAFTS
- ☐ MUSIC/SINGING
- ☐ OUTDOORS PLAY
- ☐ TV/MOVIE
- ☐ FIELD TRIP
- ☐ PLAYDATE WITH _____
- ☐ OTHER _____

SLEEP:

FROM	TO

ACCIDENT REPORT:

ACCIDENT	CARE GIVEN

MEDICATION(S):

TIME	TYPE	AMOUNT

SUPPLIES NEEDED:
_____
_____
_____
_____
_____
_____

NOTES TO PARENTS:
_____
_____
_____
_____
_____

TIME IN: TIME OUT:

TODDLER REPORT

CHILD'S NAME:

DATE:

Ⓢ Ⓜ Ⓣ Ⓦ Ⓣ Ⓕ Ⓢ

MOOD:
- ☐ Chatty
- ☐ Cranky
- ☐ Cuddly
- ☐ Friendly
- ☐ Fussy
- ☐ Grumpy
- ☐ Happy
- ☐ Playful
- ☐ Quiet
- ☐ Sad
- ☐ Sick
- ☐ Sleepy
- ☐ Other: _____

NOTES FROM PARENT(S):

WOKE UP AT:
A.M.
P.M.

LAST FED AT:
A.M.
P.M.

MEALS:

	TIME
Breakfast	
Snack	
Lunch	
Snack	
Dinner	

POTTY:

Time	Diaper	Potty	Dry	Wet	BM
	☐	☐	☐	☐	☐
	☐	☐	☐	☐	☐
	☐	☐	☐	☐	☐
	☐	☐	☐	☐	☐
	☐	☐	☐	☐	☐
	☐	☐	☐	☐	☐
	☐	☐	☐	☐	☐

ACTIVITIES:
- ☐ FREE PLAY
- ☐ READING
- ☐ ARTS/CRAFTS
- ☐ MUSIC/SINGING
- ☐ OUTDOORS PLAY
- ☐ TV/MOVIE
- ☐ FIELD TRIP
- ☐ PLAYDATE WITH _____
- ☐ OTHER _____

SLEEP:

FROM	TO

ACCIDENT REPORT:

ACCIDENT	CARE GIVEN

MEDICATION(S):

TIME	TYPE	AMOUNT

SUPPLIES NEEDED:

NOTES TO PARENTS:

TIME IN: **TIME OUT:**

TODDLER REPORT

CHILD'S NAME:

DATE:

Ⓢ Ⓜ Ⓣ Ⓦ Ⓣ Ⓕ Ⓢ

MOOD:
- ☐ Chatty
- ☐ Happy
- ☐ Cranky
- ☐ Playful
- ☐ Cuddly
- ☐ Quiet
- ☐ Friendly
- ☐ Sad
- ☐ Fussy
- ☐ Sick
- ☐ Grumpy
- ☐ Sleepy
- ☐ Other: _____

NOTES FROM PARENT(S):

WOKE UP AT:
A.M.
P.M.

LAST FED AT:
A.M.
P.M.

MEALS:

	TIME
Breakfast	
Snack	
Lunch	
Snack	
Dinner	

POTTY:

Time	Diaper	Potty	Dry	Wet	BM
	☐	☐	☐	☐	☐
	☐	☐	☐	☐	☐
	☐	☐	☐	☐	☐
	☐	☐	☐	☐	☐
	☐	☐	☐	☐	☐
	☐	☐	☐	☐	☐
	☐	☐	☐	☐	☐

ACTIVITIES:
- ☐ FREE PLAY
- ☐ READING
- ☐ ARTS/CRAFTS
- ☐ MUSIC/SINGING
- ☐ OUTDOORS PLAY
- ☐ TV/MOVIE
- ☐ FIELD TRIP
- ☐ PLAYDATE WITH _____
- ☐ OTHER _____

SLEEP:

FROM	TO

ACCIDENT REPORT:

ACCIDENT	CARE GIVEN

MEDICATION(S):

TIME	TYPE	AMOUNT

SUPPLIES NEEDED:

NOTES TO PARENTS:

TIME IN:

TIME OUT:

TODDLER REPORT

CHILD'S NAME:

DATE:

Ⓢ Ⓜ Ⓣ Ⓦ Ⓣ Ⓕ Ⓢ

MOOD:
- ☐ Chatty
- ☐ Happy
- ☐ Cranky
- ☐ Playful
- ☐ Cuddly
- ☐ Quiet
- ☐ Friendly
- ☐ Sad
- ☐ Fussy
- ☐ Sick
- ☐ Grumpy
- ☐ Sleepy
- ☐ Other: _____

NOTES FROM PARENT(S):

WOKE UP AT:
A.M.
P.M.

LAST FED AT:
A.M.
P.M.

MEALS:

	TIME
Breakfast	
Snack	
Lunch	
Snack	
Dinner	

POTTY:

Time	Diaper	Potty	Dry	Wet	BM
____	☐	☐	☐	☐	☐
____	☐	☐	☐	☐	☐
____	☐	☐	☐	☐	☐
____	☐	☐	☐	☐	☐
____	☐	☐	☐	☐	☐
____	☐	☐	☐	☐	☐
____	☐	☐	☐	☐	☐

ACTIVITIES:
- ☐ FREE PLAY
- ☐ READING
- ☐ ARTS/CRAFTS
- ☐ MUSIC/SINGING
- ☐ OUTDOORS PLAY
- ☐ TV/MOVIE
- ☐ FIELD TRIP
- ☐ PLAYDATE WITH _____
- ☐ OTHER _____

SLEEP:

FROM	TO

ACCIDENT REPORT:

ACCIDENT	CARE GIVEN

MEDICATION(S):

TIME	TYPE	AMOUNT

SUPPLIES NEEDED:

NOTES TO PARENTS:

TIME IN: **TIME OUT:**

TODDLER REPORT

CHILD'S NAME:

DATE:

Ⓢ Ⓜ Ⓣ Ⓦ Ⓣ Ⓕ Ⓢ

MOOD:
- ☐ Chatty
- ☐ Happy
- ☐ Cranky
- ☐ Playful
- ☐ Cuddly
- ☐ Quiet
- ☐ Friendly
- ☐ Sad
- ☐ Fussy
- ☐ Sick
- ☐ Grumpy
- ☐ Sleepy
- ☐ Other: _____

NOTES FROM PARENT(S):
_____
_____
_____
_____
_____

WOKE UP AT:
A.M.
P.M.

LAST FED AT:
A.M.
P.M.

MEALS:

	TIME
Breakfast	
Snack	
Lunch	
Snack	
Dinner	

POTTY:

Time	Diaper	Potty	Dry	Wet	BM
____	☐	☐	☐	☐	☐
____	☐	☐	☐	☐	☐
____	☐	☐	☐	☐	☐
____	☐	☐	☐	☐	☐
____	☐	☐	☐	☐	☐
____	☐	☐	☐	☐	☐
____	☐	☐	☐	☐	☐

ACTIVITIES:
- ☐ FREE PLAY
- ☐ READING
- ☐ ARTS/CRAFTS
- ☐ MUSIC/SINGING
- ☐ OUTDOORS PLAY
- ☐ TV/MOVIE
- ☐ FIELD TRIP
- ☐ PLAYDATE WITH _____
- ☐ OTHER _____

SLEEP:

FROM	TO

ACCIDENT REPORT:

ACCIDENT	CARE GIVEN

MEDICATION(S):

TIME	TYPE	AMOUNT

SUPPLIES NEEDED:
_____
_____
_____
_____
_____
_____

NOTES TO PARENTS:
_____
_____
_____
_____
_____
_____

TIME IN: TIME OUT:

TODDLER REPORT

CHILD'S NAME:

DATE:

Ⓢ Ⓜ Ⓣ Ⓦ Ⓣ Ⓕ Ⓢ

MOOD:
- ☐ Chatty
- ☐ Cranky
- ☐ Cuddly
- ☐ Friendly
- ☐ Fussy
- ☐ Grumpy
- ☐ Happy
- ☐ Playful
- ☐ Quiet
- ☐ Sad
- ☐ Sick
- ☐ Sleepy
- ☐ Other: _____

NOTES FROM PARENT(S):
_____
_____
_____
_____

WOKE UP AT:
A.M.
P.M.

LAST FED AT:
A.M.
P.M.

MEALS:

	TIME
Breakfast	
Snack	
Lunch	
Snack	
Dinner	

POTTY:

Time	Diaper	Potty	Dry	Wet	BM
_____	☐	☐	☐	☐	☐
_____	☐	☐	☐	☐	☐
_____	☐	☐	☐	☐	☐
_____	☐	☐	☐	☐	☐
_____	☐	☐	☐	☐	☐
_____	☐	☐	☐	☐	☐
_____	☐	☐	☐	☐	☐

ACTIVITIES:
- ☐ FREE PLAY
- ☐ READING
- ☐ ARTS/CRAFTS
- ☐ MUSIC/SINGING
- ☐ OUTDOORS PLAY
- ☐ TV/MOVIE
- ☐ FIELD TRIP
- ☐ PLAYDATE WITH _____
- ☐ OTHER _____

SLEEP:

FROM	TO

ACCIDENT REPORT:

ACCIDENT	CARE GIVEN

MEDICATION(S):

TIME	TYPE	AMOUNT

SUPPLIES NEEDED:
_____
_____
_____
_____

NOTES TO PARENTS:
_____
_____
_____
_____
_____

TIME IN: **TIME OUT:**

TODDLER REPORT

CHILD'S NAME: _____

DATE: _____

Ⓢ Ⓜ Ⓣ Ⓦ Ⓣ Ⓕ Ⓢ

MOOD:
- ☐ Chatty
- ☐ Happy
- ☐ Cranky
- ☐ Playful
- ☐ Cuddly
- ☐ Quiet
- ☐ Friendly
- ☐ Sad
- ☐ Fussy
- ☐ Sick
- ☐ Grumpy
- ☐ Sleepy
- ☐ Other: _____

NOTES FROM PARENT(S):
_____
_____
_____
_____

WOKE UP AT:
_____ A.M.
_____ P.M.

LAST FED AT:
_____ A.M.
_____ P.M.

MEALS:

	TIME
Breakfast	
Snack	
Lunch	
Snack	
Dinner	

POTTY:

Time	Diaper	Potty	Dry	Wet	BM
	☐	☐	☐	☐	☐
	☐	☐	☐	☐	☐
	☐	☐	☐	☐	☐
	☐	☐	☐	☐	☐
	☐	☐	☐	☐	☐
	☐	☐	☐	☐	☐
	☐	☐	☐	☐	☐

ACTIVITIES:
- ☐ FREE PLAY
- ☐ READING
- ☐ ARTS/CRAFTS
- ☐ MUSIC/SINGING
- ☐ OUTDOORS PLAY
- ☐ TV/MOVIE
- ☐ FIELD TRIP
- ☐ PLAYDATE WITH _____
- ☐ OTHER _____

SLEEP:

FROM	TO

ACCIDENT REPORT:

ACCIDENT	CARE GIVEN

MEDICATION(S):

TIME	TYPE	AMOUNT

SUPPLIES NEEDED:
_____
_____
_____
_____
_____

NOTES TO PARENTS:
_____
_____
_____
_____
_____

TIME IN: _____ TIME OUT: _____

TODDLER REPORT

CHILD'S NAME:

DATE:

Ⓢ Ⓜ Ⓣ Ⓦ Ⓣ Ⓕ Ⓢ

MOOD:
- ☐ Chatty
- ☐ Happy
- ☐ Cranky
- ☐ Playful
- ☐ Cuddly
- ☐ Quiet
- ☐ Friendly
- ☐ Sad
- ☐ Fussy
- ☐ Sick
- ☐ Grumpy
- ☐ Sleepy
- ☐ Other: _____

NOTES FROM PARENT(S):
_____
_____
_____
_____
_____

WOKE UP AT:
A.M.
P.M.

LAST FED AT:
A.M.
P.M.

MEALS:

	TIME
Breakfast	
Snack	
Lunch	
Snack	
Dinner	

POTTY:

Time	Diaper	Potty	Dry	Wet	BM
____	☐	☐	☐	☐	☐
____	☐	☐	☐	☐	☐
____	☐	☐	☐	☐	☐
____	☐	☐	☐	☐	☐
____	☐	☐	☐	☐	☐
____	☐	☐	☐	☐	☐
____	☐	☐	☐	☐	☐

ACTIVITIES:
- ☐ FREE PLAY
- ☐ READING
- ☐ ARTS/CRAFTS
- ☐ MUSIC/SINGING
- ☐ OUTDOORS PLAY
- ☐ TV/MOVIE
- ☐ FIELD TRIP
- ☐ PLAYDATE WITH _____
- ☐ OTHER _____

SLEEP:

FROM	TO

ACCIDENT REPORT:

ACCIDENT	CARE GIVEN

MEDICATION(S):

TIME	TYPE	AMOUNT

SUPPLIES NEEDED:
_____
_____
_____
_____
_____

NOTES TO PARENTS:
_____
_____
_____
_____
_____
_____

TIME IN: **TIME OUT:**

TODDLER REPORT

CHILD'S NAME:

DATE:

Ⓢ Ⓜ Ⓣ Ⓦ Ⓣ Ⓕ Ⓢ

MOOD:
- ☐ Chatty
- ☐ Cranky
- ☐ Cuddly
- ☐ Friendly
- ☐ Fussy
- ☐ Grumpy
- ☐ Happy
- ☐ Playful
- ☐ Quiet
- ☐ Sad
- ☐ Sick
- ☐ Sleepy
- ☐ Other: _____

NOTES FROM PARENT(S):

WOKE UP AT:
A.M.
P.M.

LAST FED AT:
A.M.
P.M.

MEALS:

	TIME
Breakfast	
Snack	
Lunch	
Snack	
Dinner	

POTTY:

Time	Diaper	Potty	Dry	Wet	BM
	☐	☐	☐	☐	☐
	☐	☐	☐	☐	☐
	☐	☐	☐	☐	☐
	☐	☐	☐	☐	☐
	☐	☐	☐	☐	☐
	☐	☐	☐	☐	☐
	☐	☐	☐	☐	☐

ACTIVITIES:
- ☐ FREE PLAY
- ☐ READING
- ☐ ARTS/CRAFTS
- ☐ MUSIC/SINGING
- ☐ OUTDOORS PLAY
- ☐ TV/MOVIE
- ☐ FIELD TRIP
- ☐ PLAYDATE WITH _____
- ☐ OTHER _____

SLEEP:

FROM	TO

ACCIDENT REPORT:

ACCIDENT	CARE GIVEN

MEDICATION(S):

TIME	TYPE	AMOUNT

SUPPLIES NEEDED:

NOTES TO PARENTS:

TIME IN: **TIME OUT:**

TODDLER REPORT

CHILD'S NAME:

DATE:

Ⓢ Ⓜ Ⓣ Ⓦ Ⓣ Ⓕ Ⓢ

MOOD:
- ☐ Chatty
- ☐ Cranky
- ☐ Cuddly
- ☐ Friendly
- ☐ Fussy
- ☐ Grumpy
- ☐ Happy
- ☐ Playful
- ☐ Quiet
- ☐ Sad
- ☐ Sick
- ☐ Sleepy
- ☐ Other: _____

NOTES FROM PARENT(S):

WOKE UP AT:
A.M.
P.M.

LAST FED AT:
A.M.
P.M.

MEALS:

	TIME
Breakfast	
Snack	
Lunch	
Snack	
Dinner	

POTTY:

Time	Diaper	Potty	Dry	Wet	BM
	☐	☐	☐	☐	☐
	☐	☐	☐	☐	☐
	☐	☐	☐	☐	☐
	☐	☐	☐	☐	☐
	☐	☐	☐	☐	☐
	☐	☐	☐	☐	☐
	☐	☐	☐	☐	☐

ACTIVITIES:
- ☐ FREE PLAY
- ☐ READING
- ☐ ARTS/CRAFTS
- ☐ MUSIC/SINGING
- ☐ OUTDOORS PLAY
- ☐ TV/MOVIE
- ☐ FIELD TRIP
- ☐ PLAYDATE WITH _____
- ☐ OTHER _____

SLEEP:

FROM	TO

ACCIDENT REPORT:

ACCIDENT	CARE GIVEN

MEDICATION(S):

TIME	TYPE	AMOUNT

SUPPLIES NEEDED:

NOTES TO PARENTS:

TIME IN: **TIME OUT:**

Made in the USA
Las Vegas, NV
29 April 2025